KU-209-164

In the Mirror
of the Past

By the same author

Celebration of Awareness

Deschooling Society

Tools for Conviviality

Energy and Equity

Limits to Medicine:
Medical Nemesis — The Expropriation of Health

Disabling Professions

The Right to Useful Unemployment

Shadow Work

Gender

H_2O and the Waters of Forgetfulness

ABC: The Alphabetization
of the Popular Mind
(with Barry Sanders)

IVAN ILLICH

In the Mirror of the Past

Lectures and Addresses
1978–1990

Marion Boyars
New York · London

Published in the United States and Great Britain in 1992
by Marion Boyars Publishers
237 East 39th Street, New York, New York 10016
24 Lacy Road, London SW15 1NL
Distributed in the United States and Canada by
Rizzoli International Publications Inc, New York

Distributed in Australia by
Peribo Pty Ltd., Terrey Hills, NSW

© Ivan Illich 1992
Copyright owner, Valentina Borremans

No part of this publication may be reproduced, stored in a retrieval system or
transmitted in any form or by any means, electronic, mechanical, photocopying,
recording or otherwise except brief extracts for the purposes of review, without
prior permission of the publishers.

Any paperback edition of this book whether published simultaneously with, or
subsequent to, the casebound edition is sold subject to the condition that it shall
not by way of trade, be lent, resold, hired out or
otherwise disposed of without the publishers' consent, in any form of binding or
cover other than that in which it was published.

The right of Ivan Illich to be identified as author of this work
has been asserted by him in accordance with the
Copyright, Designs and Patents Act 1988.

British Library Cataloguing in Publication Data
Illich, Ivan *1926–*
    In the mirror of the past : lectures and addresses 1978–
1990.
    1. United States.   English prose
    I. Title
    814.52

Library of Congress Cataloging-in-Publication Data
Illich, Ivan, 1926–
    In the mirror of the past : lectures and addresses, 1978–1990 /
Ivan Illich.
    Includes bibliographical references.
        1. Illich, Ivan, 1926–   . 2. Education—
    Philosophy.   3. Social problems.   4. Medicine—
Philosophy.   I. Title.
    LB885.I4415   1991
    370'.1—dc20   91-18898

ISBN: 0–7145–2937–0 Cloth

Printed in Great Britain by
Billing & Sons Ltd, Worcester

Table of Contents

PART THREE

PART FOUR

Introduction

This volume contains notes that I prepared for my interventions at public meetings held between 1978 and 1990. The manuscripts were selected by Valentina Borremans who also decided upon their sequence. Some have been previously published, others appear here for the first time. Their original purpose explains their style, the occasional duplication of arguments and the absence of references.

From my lecture notes, Valentina Borremans has selected only those which were prepared for meetings held in English and which, in addition, manifest a special concern of mine: each was written as a plea addressed to a different audience and each argues for the historical review of a seemingly trivial notion. In each instance I plead for a historical perspective on precisely those assumptions that are accepted as verities or 'practical certainties' as long as their sociogenesis remains unexamined.

In some of these lectures I address professionals. The fact that I was invited by them made me suspect that the fundamental issues that undermine the self-image of the group were on the hidden agenda. In each instance I attempted to call attention to the axioms that generate that epoch-specific mental space within which both everyday and professional reality has come into existence.

My own reading and teaching during the last several years was mainly concerned with mid-twelfth-century imagination, perception, conceptions and fantasy. By interpreting texts of Hugh of Saint-Victor, Heloise, Guibert and Theophilus Presbyter, I tried to grasp the occasional, premature emergence of a kind of assumption whose descendants have become a social reality that we no longer dare wish away. My public lectures were a distraction from these medieval studies and the reader will notice that not infrequently I look at the present as if I had to report on it to the authors of the old texts I try to understand. To each audience I wanted to suggest that only in the mirror of the past does it become possible to recognize the radical otherness of our twentieth-century mental topology and to become aware of its generative axioms that usually remain below the horizon of contemporary attention.

To most of the meetings, for which I prepared these notes, I was invited, often explicitly, as a welcome outsider whose writings, decades ago, had been controversial among the older members of the assembly. I never accepted any invitation unless my host understood that a long route, which could not be compressed into a few introductory remarks of a lecture, separated my current concerns from the books and pamphlets crafted by a much younger man. I showed both prudence and respect for the inviting profession by abstaining from the special language that gave the tone to the particular gathering, be it that of architects, educators, policy makers, medical personnel, Lutheran bishops, or economists. In each case I saw it as my task to fuel controversy on precisely those concepts, sense perceptions or moral convictions that, within the particular circle I was addressing, were probably taboo. On each occasion I lampoon the shibboleths of the year.

The notes from my files are here arranged without regard to their chronological sequence. This obscures the progress of my thought and terminology, but it might make it easier for the reader to grasp the main thread.

In Part One I sketch out what I mean by the 'commons', and how I perceive traditional culture as that set of rules which prevented the expansion of scarcity perceptions within a community. I do so first by separating peace from development and then by recognizing the alternative to this de-linkage as something about which I could not speak. Thirdly, I clarify that the alternative to economics cannot be reduced to alternative economics. What is lost when the commons are turned into resources is then exemplified in the notes on silence and dwelling. In the address to the Japanese Entropy Society, I argue that it is the social creation of disvalue which forces us into economic activities and growth. In the last note of this first section, I deal with the dimensions of public option, with a view toward checking the further expansion of disvalue. I search for the politics of renunciation by which, even beyond the ages of culture, desire may flourish and needs decline.

The next chapters in Part Two are addressed to so-called educators. Their common theme is a plea for research *on* education rather than *in* education. In different ways, I ask for research on those verities which constitute the common latent assumptions of current educational theories. I argue that the educational sphere is no less a social construct than what was called the sub-lunar sphere, or that of Venus. I suggest that the sociogenesis of *homo educandus* ought to be studied in the way Louis Dumont studied the emergence of *homo oeconomicus*. I argue that the assumption of mother tongue or of man's 'natural' destination to begin life as mono-lingual has a recognizable beginning and thus might also come to an end.

At this point my inquiry in Part Three leads into the 'history of stuff'. What I mean by the 'stuff' of modernity appears from a reflection on water turned into H_2O. The next chapters are for me reminders of a transitional period which led me from the study of schooling as a mythopoetic liturgy, or ritual, to the transformation of the West under the symbolic impact of the alphabet. I recount my steps and call for research on the symbolic effectiveness of notational systems on the sense perceptions of those who cannot manipulate them. The detachment of the 'text' from the manuscript page around the year 1170 generates the new literate stuff that jells into verities and memories. But that stuff too is unstable. What I call 'lay literacy' in the twelfth century becomes for me a metaphor for the 'cybernetic trance' which the use of computers can induce not only in their operators but in the computer-illiterate as well.

In 1976 I published the third and last version of *Medical*

Nemesis, and spent six weeks arguing about it. Since then I have abstained from all discussions with health profession- als. In Part Four I argue that health care is certainly no longer the key issue. I still do not understand how it could have been taken so seriously. The perception of 'life' as the ultimate resource and its insidious management are the themes we ought to explore. This is the point for a call to debunk bio-ethics which I drafted in company with Dr Robert Mendelsohn. He died before signing it.

Some of these papers are, in content and form, the result of my longstanding collaboration with Lee Hoinacki. I dedicate this volume to Marion Boyars, the publisher of all my books in English, and a friend whose criticism and encouragement I treasure.

Ivan Illich,
Ocotepec, 1991

PART ONE

The De-linking of Peace and Development

Opening address on the occasion of
the first meeting of the
Asian Peace Research Association
Yokohama, 1st December 1980

Professor Yoshikazu Sakamoto. Your invitation to open this series of keynote speeches on the occasion of the foundation of the Asian Peace Research Association both honors and frightens me. I thank you for such trust, but also beg your forbearance for my ignorance of things Japanese. This is the first time that I have given a public speech in a country of whose language I am totally ignorant.

You have invited me to speak on a subject which eludes the modern use of certain English terms. Violence now lurks in many key words of the English language. John F. Kennedy could wage *war* on poverty; pacifists now plan *strategies* (literally, war plans) for peace. In this language, currently shaped for aggression, I must talk to you about the recovery of a true sense of peace, while bearing in mind always that I know nothing about your vernacular tongue. Therefore, each word I speak today will remind me of the difficulty of putting peace into words. To me, it seems that each people's peace is as distinct as each people's poetry. Hence, the translation of peace is a task as arduous as the translation of poetry.

Peace has a different meaning for each epoch and for each culture area. This is a point on which Professor Takeshi Ishida has written. And, as he reminds us, within each culture area peace means something different both at the center and on the margins. At the center, the emphasis is on 'peace keeping'; on the margin, people hope to be 'left in peace.' During three so-called Development Decades, the latter meaning, *people's peace*, has lost out. This is my main thesis: under the cover of 'development,' a worldwide war has been waged against people's peace. In developed areas today, not much is left of the people's peace. I believe that limits to economic development, originating at the grass roots, are the principal condition for people to recover their peace.

Culture has always given meaning to peace. Each *ethnos* — people, community, culture — has been mirrored, symbolically expressed and reinforced by its own *ethos* — myth, law, goddess, ideal — of peace. Peace is as vernacular as speech. In the examples chosen by Professor Ishida, this correspondence between *ethnos* and *ethos* appears with great clarity. Take the Jews; look at the Jewish patriarch when he raises his arms in blessing over his family and flock. He invokes *shalom*, which we translate as peace. He sees shalom as grace, flowing from heaven, 'like oil dripping through the beard of Aaron the forefather.' For the Semitic father, peace is the blessing of justice which the one true God pours over the twelve tribes of recently settled shepherds.

To the Jew, the angel announces *shalom*, not the Roman *pax*. Roman peace means something utterly different. When the Roman governor raises the ensign of his legion to ram it into the soil of Palestine, he does not look toward heaven. He faces a far-off city; he imposes *its* law and *its* order. There is nothing in common between *shalom* and this *pax romana*, though both exist in the same place and time.

In our time, both have faded. *Shalom* has retired into a privatized realm of religion, and *pax* has invaded the world as 'peace' — *paix, pace*. Through two thousand years of use by governing élites, *pax* has become a polemical catchall. The term was exploited by Constantine to turn the cross into ideology. Charlemagne utilized it to justify the genocide of the Saxons. *Pax* was the term employed by Innocent III to subject the sword to the cross. In modern times, leaders manipulate it to put the party in control of the army. Spoken by both St Francis and Clemenceau, *pax* has now lost the boundaries of its meaning. It has become a sectarian and proselytizing term, whether used by the establishment or by dissidents, whether its legitimacy is claimed by the East or the West.

The idea of *pax* has a colorful history, in spite of the fact that little research has been done on it. Historians have been more occupied filling library shelves with treatises on war and its techniques. *Huo'ping* and *Shanti* seem to have meanings today which are not unlike those of the past. But between them there is a gulf; they are not comparable at all. The *Huo'ping* of the Chinese means smooth, tranquil harmony within the hierarchy of the heavens, while the *Shanti* of the Indians refers primarily to intimate, personal, cosmic, non-hierarchic awakening. In short, there is no 'identity' in peace.

In its concrete sense, peace places the 'I' within the corresponding 'we'. But in each language area, this correspondence is different. Peace fixes the meaning of the first person plural. By defining the form of the *exclusive* 'we' (the *kami* of the Malay languages), peace is the base on which the *inclusive* 'we' (the *kita*) of the Malay languages comes naturally to most speakers around the Pacific. It is a grammatical difference utterly foreign to Europe, and completely lacking in Western *pax*. Modern Europe's undifferentiated 'we' is semantically aggressive. Therefore, Asian research cannot be too wary of *pax*, which has no respect for *kita*, the *Adat*. Here in the Far East it should be easier than in the West to base peace research on what ought perhaps to be its fundamental axiom: war tends to make cultures alike whereas peace is that condition under which each culture flowers in its own incomparable way. From this it follows that peace cannot be exported; it is inevitably corrupted by transfer, its attempted export means war. When peace research neglects this ethnological truism, it turns into a technology of peace keeping: either degraded into some kind of moral rearmament, or perverted into the negative polemology (war science) of the high brass and their computer games.

Peace remains unreal, merely an abstraction, unless it stands for an ethno-anthropological reality. But it would remain equally unreal if we did not attend to its historical dimension. Until quite recently, war could not totally destroy peace, could not penetrate all of its levels, because the continuation of war was based on the survival of the subsistence cultures which fed it. Traditional warfare depended on the continuation of people's peace. Too many historians have neglected this fact; they make history appear as a tale of wars. This is clearly true of classical historians, who tend to report on the rise and fall of the powerful. Unfortunately, it is equally true for many of the newer historians who want to act as reporters from the camps of those who never made it, who want to tell the tales of the vanquished, to evoke the images of those who have disappeared. Too often these new historians are more interested in the violence than the peace of the poor. They primarily chronicle resistance, mutinies, insurgencies, riots of slaves, peasants, minorities, marginals; in more recent times, the class struggles of proletarians and the discrimination battles of women.

In comparison with the historians of power, the new historians of popular culture have a difficult task. Historians of élite cultures, of wars waged by armies, write about the centers of cultural areas. For their documentation they have monuments, decrees engraved in stone, commercial correspondence, the autobiographies of kings and the firm trails made by marching armies. Historians from the losing camp have no evidence of this kind. They report on subjects which often have been erased from the face of the earth, on people whose remains have been stamped out by their enemies, or blown away by the wind. The historians of peasantry and nomads, of village culture and home life, of women and infants, have few traces to examine. They must reconstruct the past from hunches, must be attentive to hints which they find in proverbs, riddles and songs. Often the only verbatim records left behind by the poor, especially women, are the responses made by witches and rogues under torture, statements recorded by the courts. Modern anthropological history (the history of popular cultures, *l'histoire des mentalités*) has had to develop techniques to make these odd remnants intelligible.

But this new history often tends to focus on war. It portrays the weak principally in their confrontations with those against whom they must defend themselves. It recounts stories of resistance and only by implication reports on the peace of the past. Conflict makes opponents comparable; it introduces simplicity into the past; it fosters the illusion that what has gone before can be related in twentieth-century uniquack. Thus war, which makes cultures alike, is all too often used by historians as the framework or skeleton of their narratives. Today there is a desperate need for the history of peace, a history infinitely more diverse than the story of war.

What is now designated as peace research very often lacks historical perspective. The subject of this research is 'peace' purged of its cultural and historical components. Paradoxically, peace was turned into an academic subject just when it had been reduced to a balance between sovereign, economic powers acting under the assumption of scarcity. Thus study is restricted to research on the least violent truce between competitors locked into a zero-sum game. Like searchlights, the concepts of this research focus on scarcity. But in the process of such research, the peaceful enjoyment of that which is not scarce, people's peace, is left in a zone of deep shadow.

The assumption of scarcity is fundamental to economics, and formal economics is the study of values under this assumption. But scarcity, and therefore all that can be meaningfully analyzed by formal economics, has been of marginal importance in the lives of most people through most of history. The spread of scarcity into all aspects of life can be chronicled; it has occurred in European civilization since the Middle Ages. Under the expanding assumption of scarcity, peace acquired a new meaning, one without precedent anywhere but in Europe. Peace came to mean *pax œconomica*. *Pax œconomica* is a balance between formally 'economic' powers.

The history of this new reality deserves our attention. And the process through which *pax œconomica* monopolized the meaning of peace is especially important. This is the first meaning of peace to achieve worldwide acceptance. And such a monopoly ought to be deeply worrisome. Therefore, I want to contrast *pax œconomica* with its opposite and complement, popular peace.

Since the establishment of the United Nations, peace has been progressively linked with development. Previously this linkage had been unthinkable. The novelty of it can hardly be understood by people under forty. The curious situation is more easily intelligible for those who were, like myself, adults on January 10, 1949, the day President Harry Truman announced the Point Four Program. On that day most of us met the term 'development' for the first time in its present meaning. Until then we had used 'development' to refer to species, to real estate and to moves in chess. But since then it can refer to people, to countries and to economic strategies. And in less than a generation we were flooded with conflicting development theories. By now, however, most of them are merely curiosities for collectors. You may remember, with some embarrassment, how generous people were urged to make sacrifices for a succession of programs aimed at 'raising per capita income,' 'catching up with the advanced countries,' 'overcoming dependencies.' And you now wonder at the many things once deemed worthy of export: 'achievement orientation,' 'atoms for peace,' 'jobs,' 'windmills' and, currently, 'alternative life styles' and professionally supervised 'self-help.' Each of these theoretical incursions came in waves. One brought the self-styled pragmatists who emphasized enterprise, the other would-be politicians who relied on 'conscientizing' people into the foreign ideology. Both camps agreed on growth. Both advocated rising production and increased dependence on consumption. And each camp with its sect of experts, each assembly of saviors, always linked its own scheme for development to peace. Concrete peace, by thus being linked to development, became a partisan goal. And the pursuit of peace through development became the overarching unexaminable axiom. Anyone who opposed economic growth, not this kind or that, but economic growth as such, could be denounced as an enemy of peace. Even Gandhi was cast into the role of the fool, the romantic or the psychopath. And worse, his teachings were perverted into so-called non-violent strategies for development. His peace, too, was linked to growth. *Khadi* was redefined as a 'commodity,' and non-violence as an economic weapon. The assumption of the economist, that values are not worth protecting unless they are scarce, has turned *pax œconomica* into a threat to people's peace.

The linkage of peace to development has made it difficult to challenge the latter. Let me suggest that such a challenge should now be the main task of peace research. And the fact that development means different things to different people is no obstacle. It means one thing to trans-national corporation executives, another to ministers of the Warsaw Pact, and something else again to the architects of the New International Economic Order. But the convergence of all parties on the need for development has given the notion a new status. This agreement has made development the condition for the pursuit of the nineteenth-century ideals of equality and democracy, with the proviso that these be restricted within the assumptions of scarcity. Under the disputes around the issue of 'who gets what' the unavoidable costs inherent in all development have been buried. But during the seventies one part of these costs has come to light. Some obvious 'truths' suddenly become controversial. Under the ecology label, the limits of resources, of tolerable poison and stress, become political issues. But the violent aggression against the environment's utilization value has so far not been sufficiently disenterred. To expose the violence against subsistence which is implicit in all further growth, and which is veiled by *pax œconomica*, seems to me a prime task of radical peace research.

In both theory and practice all development means the transformation of subsistence-oriented cultures and their integration into an economic system. Development always entails the expansion of a formally economic sphere at the expense of subsistence-oriented activities. It means the progressive 'disembedding' of a sphere in which exchange takes place under the assumption of a zero-sum game. And this expansion proceeds at the cost of all other traditional forms of exchange.

Thus development always implies the propagation of scarcity-dependence on goods and services perceived as scarce. Development necessarily creates a milieu from which the conditions for subsistence activities have been eliminated in the process of making the milieu over into a resource for the production and circulation of commodities. Development thus inevitably means the imposition of *pax œconomica* at the cost of every form of popular peace.

To illustrate the opposition between people's peace and *pax œconomica*, let me turn to the European Middle Ages. In so doing, I emphatically do not advocate a return to the past. I look at the past only to illustrate the dynamic opposition between two complementary forms of peace, both formally recognized. I explore the past rather than some social science theory in order to avoid utopian thinking and a planning mentality. The past is not, like plans and ideals, something which might possibly come about. It allows me to stand on fact when I look at the present. I turn toward the European Middle Ages because it was near their end that a violent *pax œconomica* assumed its shape. And the replacement of people's peace by its engineered counterfeit, *pax œconomica*, is one of Europe's exports.

In the twelfth century, *pax* did not mean the absence of war between lords. The *pax* that Church or Emperor wanted to guarantee was not primarily the absence of armed encounters between knights. *Pax*, for peace, meant to protect the poor and their means of subsistence from the violence of war. Peace protected the peasant and the monk. This was the meaning of *Gottesfrieden*, of *Landfrieden*. It protected specific times and places. No matter how bloody the conflict among lords, peace protected the oxen and the grain on the stem. It safeguarded the emergency granary, the seed and the time of harvest. Generally speaking, the 'peace of the land' shielded the utilization values of the common environment from violent interference. It ensured access to water and pasture, to woods and livestock, for those who had nothing else from which to draw their subsistence. The 'peace of the land' was thus distinct from the truce between warring parties. This primarily subsistence-oriented significance of peace was lost with the Renaissance.

With the rise of the nation-state, an entirely new world began to emerge. This world ushered in a new kind of peace and a new kind of violence. Both its peace and its violence are equally distant from all the forms of peace and violence which had previously existed. Whereas peace had formerly meant the protection of that minimal subsistence on which the wars among lords had to be fed, henceforth subsistence itself became the victim of an aggression, supposedly peaceful. Subsistence became the prey of expanding markets in services and goods. This new kind of peace entailed the pursuit of a utopia. Popular peace had protected precarious but real communities from total extinction. But the new peace was built around an abstraction. The new peace is cut to the measure of *homo œconomicus*, universal man, made by nature to live on the consumption of commodities produced elsewhere by others. While the *pax populi* had protected vernacular autonomy, the environment in which this could thrive and the variety of patterns for its reproduction, the new *pax œconomica* protected production. It ensures aggression against popular culture, the commons and women.

First, *pax œconomica* cloaks the assumption that people have become incapable of providing for themselves. It empowers a new élite to make all people's survival dependent on their access to education, health care, police protection, apartments and supermarkets. In ways previously unknown, it exalts the producer and degrades the consumer. *Pax œconomica* labels the subsistent as 'unproductive,' the autonomous as 'asocial,' the traditional as 'underdeveloped.' It spells violence against all local customs which do not fit a zero-sum game.

Secondly, *pax œconomica* promotes violence against the environment. The new peace guarantees impunity — the environment may be used as a resource to be mined for the production of commodities, and as a space reserved for their circulation. It does not just permit, but it encourages the destruction of the commons. People's peace had protected the commons. It guarded the poor man's access to pastures and woods; it safeguarded the use of the road and the river by people; it reserved for widows and beggars exceptional rights for utilizing the environment. *Pax œconomica* defines the environment as a scarce resource which it reserves for optimal use in the production of goods and the provision of professional care. Historically, this is what development has meant: starting from the enclosure of the lord's sheep and reaching to the enclosure of streets for the use of cars and to the restriction of desirable jobs to those with more than twelve years of schooling. Development has always signified a violent exclusion of those who wanted to survive without dependence on consumption from the environment's utilization values. *Pax œconomica* bespeaks war against the commons.

Thirdly, the new peace promotes a new kind of war between the sexes. The transition from the traditional battle for dominance to this new all-out war between men and women is probably the least analyzed of economic growth's side effects. This war, too, is a necessary outcome of the so-called growth of productive forces, a process implying an increasingly complete monopoly of wage-labor over all other forms of work. And this, too, is aggression. The monopoly of wage-related work entails aggression against a feature common to all subsistence-oriented societies. Though these societies may be as different from each other as those of Japan, France and Fiji, one central characteristic is common to all of them: all tasks relevant to subsistence are assigned in a gender-specific way, to either men or women. The set of specific tasks which are necessary and culturally defined vary from society to society. But each society distributes the various possible tasks to either men or women, and does so according to its own unique pattern. In no two cultures is the distribution of tasks within a society the same. In each culture, 'growing up' means to grow into the activities characteristic there, and only there, of either man or woman. To be a man or a woman in pre-industrial societies is not a secondary trait added on to genderless humans. It is the most fundamental characteristic in every single action. To grow up does not mean to be 'educated,' but to grow into life by acting as a woman or as a man. Dynamic peace between men and women consists of precisely this division of concrete tasks. And this does not signify equality; it establishes limits to mutual oppression. Even in this intimate domain, people's peace limits both war and the extent of domination. Wage-labor destroys this pattern.

Industrial work, productive work, is conceived as neutral and often experienced as such. It is defined as genderless work. And this is true whether it is paid or unpaid, whether its rhythm is determined by production or by consumption. But even though work is conceived as genderless, access to this activity is radically biased. Men have primary access to the paid tasks which are viewed as desirable, and women are assigned those left over. Originally, women were the ones forced into unpaid shadow work, although men are now increasingly given these tasks too. As a consequence of this neutralization of work, development inevitably promotes a new kind of war between the sexes, a competition between theoretical equals of whom half are handicapped by their sex. Now we see a competition for wage-labor, which has become scarce, and a struggle to avoid shadow work, which is neither paid nor capable of contributing to subsistence.

Pax œconomica protects a zero-sum game, and ensures its undisturbed progress. All are coerced to become players and to accept the rules of *homo œconomicus*. Those who refuse to fit the ruling model are either banished as enemies of the peace, or educated until they conform. By the rules of the zero-sum game, both the environment and human work are scarce stakes; as one gains the other loses. Peace is now reduced to two meanings: the myth that, at least in economics, two and two will one day make five, or a truce and deadlock. Development is the name given to the expansion of this game, to the incorporation of more players and of their resources. Therefore, the monopoly of *pax œconomica* must be deadly; and there must be some peace other than the one linked to development. One can concede that *pax œconomica* is not without some positive value — bicycles have been invented and their components must circulate in markets different from those in which pepper was formerly traded. And peace among economic powers is at least as important as peace between the warlords of ancient times. But the monopoly of this élite peace must be questioned. To formulate this challenge seems to me the most fundamental task of peace research today.

The Right to Dignified Silence

Address to 'People's Forum: Hope'
Tokyo, 23rd April 1982

Last winter, visitors to a certain city in Germany witnessed a quite unusual scene. At selected times, and only for one hour, some people regularly gathered at busy intersections and remained silent. They stood mute in the cold, shifting their feet now and then, not saying a word, not responding to passersby. When the hour ended, they drifted away, still silent. These quiet people were careful not to disturb traffic nor to hinder pedestrians. They wore ordinary dress. Usually one or two carried a sign which gave the reason for their stance: 'I am silent because I have nothing to say about nuclear destruction.'

I joined some of these silent groups. And I soon noticed that such quiet people can be very offensive to those who pass by — the silence of such a group speaks with irrepressible loudness. This stillness thunders, conveying inexpressible horror. Germans are well-informed about the effects of nuclear machines. The majority, however, brushes aside scientific evidence showing the unavoidable consequences of the deployment of nuclear devices. Some, honorable and religious, have reconciled themselves to the risks posed by stationing an increasing number of American Cruise and Pershing missiles on German soil. However, a sizeable and growing minority determinedly opposes further nuclear armament, and more than a few among them are committed to unconditional nuclear disarmament.

The silent people present a provocative challenge to both

hawks and the entire spectrum of doves. Those who choose to participate in the street corner ritual commit themselves to say nothing and to answer no questions. Once an irritated man kept at me for half an hour. I am sure that he supported unilateral disarmament as strongly as I, but in his view silence was not the proper way to stand up for my convictions. But I could not respond then and there.

Now, I can give four reasons for the belief, shared by many others, that it is imperative that some of us exercise nonviolent, defensive silence, even at the cost of disturbing or hurting some of our friends. I shall answer four questions: 1) Why is a response of silence to nuclear bombs so important, especially in Germany? 2) Why do I, as a philosopher, believe that argument alone is not sufficient to resist the production, stationing and maintenance of nuclear devices? 3) Why do I think that silence is often more compelling than words? 4) Why do I count silence among those human rights which deserve the protection of law?

First, I believe that young Germans have a special relationship to genocidal machines. But one must understand what a genocidal machine is; it is *not* a weapon. It is, as the atomic bomb, a fundamentally new type of phenomenon. Nuclear devices are objects with no similarity to anything built in the past. Genocide, however, is nothing new. Throughout history, conquerors often eradicated cities or whole populations. We read in the Bible, for example, that the Jews felt instructed by their God to kill every human being in certain cities they had conquered.

But our ancestors committed genocide with means which also had normal uses — clubs, knives or fire. These objects were used for peaceful purposes, for example, the preparation of food, but also for the horrendous acts of torture, murder and genocide. This is not true of atomic bombs. Their exclusive purpose is genocide. They are not useful for anything else, not even for murder.

Such genocidal instruments, inventions for the destruction of peoples, were conceived for the first time in the early forties, at the same time as President Roosevelt set out to produce the atomic bomb, following the guidelines of Albert

Einstein. Simultaneously, Hitler began research on such a bomb in Germany. Its conception there, however, created extermination camps for the mass murder of Jews, Gypsies, homosexuals and other groups of people considered unworthy of life.

These camps had been in operation for four years when the Enola Gay dropped its bomb on Hiroshima. They were operated by Germans, most of whom are now dead or quite old. However, many young Germans feel a personal association with those genocidal machines employed by some of their parents, although they were born after the last concentration camps, the last gas chambers, the last mass crematoria were shut down or torn down. These young people, haunted by the images of the camps, experience unspeakable horror. They consider it totally unnecessary and, indeed, quite impossible to state any logical reason why they would resist reconstruction of such camps. They think it unnecessary because nobody in Germany today proposes concentration camps for the purpose of genocide, and they think it impossible to discuss the obvious.

In Nazi Germany, the only ones who argued against the construction and operation of concentration camps were some high-ranking Nazi functionaries who believed either that genocide should be postponed, or that it could be carried out more effectively by other means. Still others called attention to the high costs. Today, many young Europeans refuse to behave as these Nazi functionaries. They recognize that atomic bombs are not weapons but genocidal machines, that their existence — and especially their emplacement on German soil — must be resisted, *but without wasting a single word on it.*

Secondly, I know that some people scream out in horror when they can no longer control their emotions. And there is nothing wrong with acting from a prudent heart rather than from a clear mind. But as a philosopher I know that there are compelling reasons for refusing to be drawn into a direct argument about certain topics. Jews, and some Christians, believe that they should not pronounce the name of God. Modern philosophers have discovered concepts which render the statements in which those concepts occur nonsensical. In wills, for example, the sentence beginning 'Upon my death I will. . .' is customary but nonsensical. Upon my death, I can no longer will anything.

Genocidal machine is another of those concepts to which logicians attribute 'extraordinary epistemological status.' I can speak about the atomic bomb (and in my personal opinion, equally about nuclear power plants) *only* with arguments which prove that it is a genocidal machine. However, as soon as this is proven, I cannot use the concept any longer in a sentence without dehumanizing my status as a speaker. Not even for the sake of discussion can I join in an argument in which the threat of genocide, however cautiously uttered, is considered.

Thirdly, I can only scream when I encounter people who deal with this matter by argument. And, paradoxically, screaming is closer to silence than to speech. Similar to tears, or the syllable *'OHM'*, certain ways of wailing and screaming lie, just as silence does, outside the realm of language. Yet these forms of expression can speak louder and more accurately than words.

Further, silence, framed by the scream of horror, transcends language. People from different countries and age groups who might not have a common language can speak with one voice in their silent scream.

Finally, unconditional opposition to the existence of genocidal machines as expressed in a commitment to silence is radically democratic. Let me clarify. If I assert that atomic bombs are not weapons but genocidal machines, and further argue as a scientist that nuclear energy will unavoidably endanger future generations, the weight of my arguments depends on my competence in a complex subject matter, and my credibility depends on my social standing. Public argument, especially in today's media-dominated society, cannot help but be hierarchical. But such is not true for eloquent and rationally chosen silence. The most intelligent and most experienced expert can use silence *as his last word*. And anyone in the world can choose silent protest and the demonstration of unspeakable horror as an expression of his direct and wise faith in life and in hope for his children. The decision to remain silent, the ritual of 'No, thank you,' is a voice with which a great majority can speak up with stark simplicity.

Fourth, in speaking out for silence as an example to be followed, I do not intend to discourage sensible argument which identifies the reasons for maintaining silence. But I am aware that silence threatens to introduce anarchy. He who remains silent is ungovernable. And silence proliferates. Hence, there will be attempts to break our silence. Our participation in 'peace discussions' will be demanded. A witch hunt against the silent people is even possible. At this time, then, the right to silent retreat from argument, the right to end argumentation if the participants' dignity, in their view, is jeopardized, must be claimed and defended. There is also a right to propagate horrified silence.

I Too Have Decided to Keep Silent

Read and distributed at the
20th *Evangelischer Kirchentag*
Hanover, 9th June 1983

I, too, have decided to keep silent

because I shall not be drawn into any discussion about genocide;

because nuclear bombs are not weapons; they cannot be used except for man's extermination;

because the deployment of nuclear bombs makes both peace and war senseless;

because silence here speaks better than words;

because in discussing conditions under which I would renounce using these bombs, I become a criminal;

because nuclear deterrence is folly;

because I will not threaten others with my suicide;

because the 'zone of silence' which surrounded genocide under the Nazis has been replaced by a 'zone of argument';

because only my silence speaks clearly in this zone of compulsive peace talks;

because my horrified silence cannot be used or governed;

because. . .

Cross out whatever does not fit you. Add your own reasons for silence. Circulate these.

Alternatives to Economics:
Toward a History of Waste

Address to the annual Human Economy Session
at the Eastern Economics Association Conference
Boston, 11th March 1988

My theme is the blessings which we still enjoy, in spite of economic growth; the rediscovery of the present when it moves out of the shadow which the future has cast on it during three development decades. And this is the moment, I think, to plead for research on the non-economic boon which we best discover when the hope in further so-called development fades.

I purposely speak of blessings and boons when I refer to the rediscovery of walking and cycling in lieu of transportation; of dwelling in self-generated space in lieu of claims to housing; of planting tomatoes on the balcony and meeting in bars that exclude radio and TV, of suffering without therapies and of preferring the intransitive activity of dying to monitored medicide. I do not use the word 'value.' I know how recently this economic term has slipped into our discourse to replace 'the good.' But I recognize the danger of trying to preserve the notion of the good. Today, the term 'good' characteristically denotes management; the professional 'for your own good' in the mouth of teachers, physicians and ideologues. I therefore try to recover the ideas of blessing and boon to speak about the rediscovery of joys, but also of sorrows, that I have observed in both rich and poor countries at the moment the expectation of marketable pleasures and securities comes to a crash.

The fact that blessing and even boon once had sectarian connotations does not worry me. For I want to argue that discourse about these experiences can have theoretical consistency and practical relevance only if it is conducted in a language which is devoid of economic implications, of references to productivity, needs, resources, decisions, systems, feedback, and above all, development.

I count it as a privilege that you invite me to discuss this theme among professional economists who see themselves as dissidents within their own discipline; that among you I may raise the issue of blessings — something economic language cannot grasp but only corrupt; that I may speak about an alternative to economics among academics who acknowledge in Boulding and in Kapp, in Mishan and, above all, in Schumacher their immediate ancestors, and among whom several claim to be inspired by Bateson. But I am also daunted by the challenge of submitting my thesis to this learned assembly because, as far as I can see, dissidence within economics has meant no more than the extension of the disciplinary umbrella of scarcity-related assumptions over facts and relationships that most main-liners leave untouched.

I am not an economist; instead I am something akin to a historian. I study history as an antidote to obsessive speculations about the future. For the historian the present appears as the future of the past. History heightens my sensitivity to the time-vector hidden in all our terms when we try to discuss public goods. Historical studies make me aware that most of the clear certainties by which I act, think and even perceive were neither suspected nor imaginable for the authors whose writings are my sources. I study history to become sensitive to those modern assumptions which, by going unexamined, have turned into our epoch-specific, *a priori* forms of perception. I am neither using history nor do I want to escape into history. I study the past to look out of its perspective at the axioms of that mental topology of thought and feeling which confronts me when I write or speak. And, coming out of the past and entering the present I find that most of the axioms generating my mental space are tinged with economics.

Preparing for this meeting, I read The Other Economic Summit (TOES) papers, and often reached for the book which Paul Ekins edited. Let me quote the words with which this book begins. 'Economics is at an impasse. Its instruments are blunted. Its direction is confused.' The public is indeed 'becoming skeptical and bewildered.' The American presidential campaign of 1988 mirrors this confusion. The post-war consensus about the status of economics as an accepted discipline is gone. While in the sixties economists were admired as society's astronomers, they are now consulted more like astrologers. Investment just does not bring down unemployment. Nor does growth. Inflation is endemic. No intelligent political candidate speaks about development. Majid Rahnema makes AIDS the metaphor for something which until quite recently was called 'takeoff' — that point at which a culture loses its immunity against a self-sustaining transmogrification into an economy. At this point latent HIV manifests itself as AIDS: cultural self-sustenance quickly breaks down. Everywhere poverty spreads with progress. The new book by Rist and Sabelli has an appropriate title: '*Once upon a time, there was something called development.*'

Relentlessly, TOES authors pile up the evidence for counterpurposive outcomes of monetarization. But much more importantly, they have created concepts which make these paradoxical and painful results of growth into scientific facts that can no longer be ignored by the academy. A whole set of new indicators has thus come into being. Technical criteria can now discriminate between the costly growth of goods and the growth of costly waste. But some of these new concepts make the alternative economist into an advocate for the economic colonization of housework, sex or gardening. Paradoxically, the economic demonstration of the counter-productivity of economic growth confirms the belief that what matters for human beings can be expressed in economic terms.

What I plead for is a second look at those certainties that are common to alternative economists and their dragons. In the mirror of the past their assumptions about wants, needs, values and resources are of the same ilk. It appears blatantly illogical when Ekins, on the same page, defines the aim of TOES as the provision of scientific guidance in the optimum allocation of scarce resources for the maximization of human welfare, and continues with this sentence: 'The very assumptions which form the basis of conventional economics are now unsound.' Constant repetition of the desire to place economics at the service of people and their welfare, rather than of things and their accumulation, in no way touches the very assumption of scarcity by which *homo œconomicus* is imputed needs and desires. Economists, professional or lay, official or dissident, drive home the assumption of scarcity with every utterance.

I cannot help but see the TOES papers as ads for the Macintosh, with its barbs against IBM. In ad after ad after ad I am told that the Mac is run on an operating system that is designed as if people mattered. Let me assume that this is true. For reasons which you can easily imagine, this would only make me more wary of the Mac. As much as with conventional economics, their opponents also conceive of economics within any society in analogy with the operating system of a computer. Economists know and manage the programs. Calling needs 'basic,' values 'human,' development 'personal,' demanding a 'sustainable use of resources' and a rate of growth 'moderated by cultural considerations,' economics can be whitewashed, but none of its basic assumptions are touched. Its language remains useful only to grasp that which from a cultural good has been changed into a value by being recast as a social factor which functions under the assumptions of scarcity.

Any serious critic of conventional economics is inevitably caught in a dilemma: in order to formulate the implicit and unavoidable consequences of economic growth he has to measure the cultural destruction which results from such growth in monetary terms. This then leads the critic to couch his recommendations in a language which sounds like an ad for Band-Aids, or a religious exhortation. However, it is not this, but another discovery which makes reading some of the

TOES papers fascinating for me. Now and then one of the authors turns from being a mere dissident into a true skeptic. Schumacher was one such person. Late in life he redefined intermediate technology (which he, after all, had originally named) as appropriate technology and became the initiator of a series of questions which now takes the form: 'After development, what?' Among the questioners, Kohr has been a teacher for many by suggesting that self-sustaining well-being depends on factors which only dimensional analysis can reveal; it cannot be reduced to any kind of welfare measured in quantitative terms.

James Robertson, in his TOES paper, provides a well-formulated example of a critique of economics as a field which goes far beyond a critique within the field. His article asks: 'What comes after full employment?' Full employment is by now recognized as a concept whose practical implementation is not a utopia, but an impossibility. Robertson discusses the evidence. He says that we are in the midst of jobless growth. Employment in many sectors is becoming an uneconomical way of getting work done, something similar to slavery in the past, becoming itself uneconomical. But it still serves some obvious purposes. For example, in an uneconomical and increasingly unethical way it serves to redistribute gains. But maybe it is time to disengage our perception of myriads of human activities from the reductionist normative concept of employment.

When Robertson reaches the end of his paper, where he has deconstructed the conventional current category of work, he notices that, in so doing, he has simultaneously deconstructed the discipline within which he argued: 'The age of economics has, in fact, coincided with the age of employment. It is only over the last two hundred years that employment has developed as the dominant way of organizing work. . . The question is whether economics will turn out to have been a fairly short-lived structure of reasoning . . . while employment has been the dominant form of work, or whether economists will be able to extend their discipline to deal with choices that reflect the needs and activities of real people as contrasted with those of *homo œconomicus*.'

Robertson, in this sentence, deals with economics as that discipline which formalized the mentality that prevailed in an epoch in which employment was the dominant form of work. Accepting the cogency of his reasoning, 'employment' can be replaced by other terms, for example, by 'needs.' The age of economics coincides with the progressive discovery of human needs, something which economists now define as finite, few, classifiable and universal. I want to focus on need, and deconstruct the naturalness of this concept in analogy to what Robertson does with work. What we perceive and experience as needs is a social creation even more recent than work.

What we define as needs was unknown in past epochs. Michael Ignatieff in *The Needs of Strangers* correctly criticizes my former attempts to speak of a 'History of Needs.' What in the past was homologous to our needs has a place so different within the constellation of social assumptions that the two are incomparable. A recent epistemic break marks the appearance of what we call 'need'. Therefore, we cannot trace the history, but can only examine the late modern sociogenesis of needs as we have learned to perceive them.

It is a delicate task to speak about the sociogenesis of needs. We need needs — our own and those of strangers — to keep our integrity intact. We must try to find a line of reasoning which avoids conjuring up either anger or nostalgia. When, for instance, I contrast the death of an old man in the corner of his hovel with the death of one whose 'needs' for intensive care have been fully met, I do not compare the desirability of two conditions or situations. The example only stresses the impossibility of using the same words when speaking about both men. Please note what I am saying. I hunt for no lessons in the past. But I believe that history, when properly practiced, makes us more clearsighted about the condition of Needy Man which *homo œconomicus* is.

Only quite recently have we begun to tolerate the definition of persons in terms of their needs. Looking at the second volume of the Oxford English Dictionary Supplement confirms this. Under the entry 'need, a substantive', the 1976 Supplement lists a new meaning: 'Psychol: A state of physiological or psychological want, that consciously or subconsciously motivates behavior toward its satisfaction.' The first quotation that is given by the dictionary to support this new, modern usage is dated 1929. Now, fifty years later, it would be difficult to use the word 'need' and prescind from this connotation. Needs have by now become motivating wants.

Then, according to the Oxford English Dictionary, the sixties added words like 'needs test,' 'needs analysis' and 'need pattern.' These neologisms indicate that needs are lacks that can be operationally verified and managed. They now constitute a lack which I recognize in the other, and which may be certified by one of the many specialized experts in needs recognition. Increasingly, my own needs are legitimate if they can also be identified in others.

Since 1960 needing has become a learning goal. Education in needing has become an increasingly prominent task. Physicians no longer confine themselves to defining the needs of a patient. They accept the 'duty' of *educating* the patient. The patient must now recognize as his own the needs which are diagnosed. This is the root meaning of 'informed consent and compliance to the therapy recommended.' Equally, social workers are no longer satisfied with the administration of their client's needs. They are trained to bring these needs to consciousness and to advocate their translation into claims. This management of the formation rather than just the satisfaction of needs is a preparation to move social policy-making beyond mere welfare. Since needs can be managed, no needs shall arise in the coming utopia that cannot realistically be satisfied by collective action. By passing from the mere imputation and management of satisfaction to the felt incarnation of needs, the service professions attempt to give leadership on the route to a Skinnered Eden.

Finally, during the seventies, the term 'basic needs' has come into economics. And in this way it became a political keyword. A new breed of economists elaborated policy recommendations based on the ethics of effective need satisfaction. The proponents of this new, ethically based economic order are consistently under attack by hard-nosed economic technicians. However, they are rarely criticized for their methods of imputing needs, or for using needs as measures of potential demand. They are usually labeled socialist, an epithet which designates someone who translates imputed needs into precise entitlements that can be used to measure the obligations incumbent on others.

What is at issue here are not the technical, mathematical ways in which various schools of economists have given expression to something which in ordinary language is now referred to as needs, but the use of this term in ordinary discourse. Not only in political debates, but also in casual conversation, unmet 'needs' are increasingly used in the definition of persons. And this began only a few years ago. The birthday of the 'under-developed' — the extremely needy — is the 10th of January 1949, when President Harry Truman brought him into existence in the speech with which he launched the Point Four program. Other analogous definitions-by-the-negative have slipped into the language in a more surreptitious way. Illiteracy, as a noun, was first used in Boston in 1982 in the *Harvard Educational Review*. Since then, statistical entities like the 'undiagnosed', 'the untreated' and 'the uninsured' have jelled into subjects with professionally definable needs and claims.

The use of needs, then, to define the human condition has become axiomatic. The human is perceived as the animal in need. The ultimate consequence of the transmogrification of cultures into economics, of goods into values, is the disembedding of the individual self. It then seems natural to define the person by abstract deficiencies rather than by peculiarity of context.

This perception of the human as a needy being constitutes a radical break with any known tradition. And a similar situation obtains with the meaning currently attributed to equality, a definition based on this 'miserable' view. Within the needs discourse, human equality is anchored in the certainty of the identity of all peoples' basic needs. We are no longer equal because of the intrinsic dignity and worth of each person, but because of the legitimacy of the claim to the recognition of a lack.

The needs-defined discourse also characterizes our alienation from each other. We live among strangers who are no less strangers for the fact that we feel responsibility toward the financing of one another's care. Needs, translated into demands, mediate our responsibility *for* the other. But it is just this which exempts us from responsibility *to* him. An example clarifies the issue:

In Japan, the assumption that people need special care because they have become old, sick or unbalanced was far from general in 1985. During that year, Mrs Hashimoto from the United Nations University contrasted two comparable communities, one in the USA and one in Japan. In Japan 70 percent of the old as against 26 in the USA live with their children, and of these, 66 percent (as against six in the USA) live in three- or four-generation households. This will not surprise anyone acquainted with Japanese family traditions. In Japan, marriage adds a new member to the household and, unlike our tradition, leaves the structure of the household intact. As a consequence, it is not surprising that in Japan formal care targets only exceptional cases of proven needs, while in the USA it targets all the old whose needs and consequent entitlements are assumed as a matter of course. What is startling for me in Hashimoto's analysis of her interviews is this: in the USA, those few families that do shelter their own after the age of 65 insist that they provide informal 'care' to old people in view of those persons' special needs. In Japan, the old simply live in the household, regardless of any perception of their needs. The old are given something best described as 'hospitality,' but they 'need' neither formal nor informal hospitalization or care.

Notwithstanding the high levels of modernization in Japan, most parents with children over 35 count on the blessing of old age within the household. Economists can calculate how much is saved by domestic care in comparison with what a bed and upkeep in an old people's home would cost. However, the language of economics is unfit to express either the boon or the burden experienced daily in the four-generation household by its members. Economic indicators can only measure abstractions, comparing phenomena in Tampa with those in Yokohama. By definition, they miss the joys and sorrows possible in a culture. The consequences of utility choices made by an economic actor under the assumption of scarcity are something quite different from the immediacy of loving this person. The latter experience results in blessings whose range runs from the heights of laughter to the sad bitterness of tears.

The needs discourse uproots grandmother from the household of which she had so far been a part, as much as the urn with an ancestor's ashes. When she is then turned into a subject within the needs discourse, a new person, a *senex œconomicus* comes into being. This new person is a stranger who by somebody's choice is hospitalized in her own bed. The household henceforth is experienced as a center of care. Grandmother from now on receives what she needs as an old woman. She no longer simply receives her due, irrespective of any claim based on an economically definable need.

During the early eighties, the needs discourse disembedded millions of elderly Japanese from the context of experience which up to then had defined both their status and the household. Even the current Japanese economy is unprepared to meet the needs which were created by this reinterpretation of age within an economic rather than a cultural context. Last year a high-level Japanese mission journeyed to Mexico. It came to negotiate an agreement which would allow Japanese enterprises to open one million beds for the disposal of aging Japanese in a tropical climate, and offered in exchange an industrial development package. The elderly, formerly experienced as a boon and a burden within the household, were turned into a disvalue for the economy. Professor Ui Jun claims that the major contribution since 1970 which poor countries have made to the Japanese economy has been the provision of opportunities for the disposal of waste and other forms of disvalue.

What I have characterized as the transformation of a culture into an economy is usually discussed in terms of the growing monetarization of the society. For a couple of decades I have pleaded that the process be studied in terms of the shadow which spreading economic structures throw over the non-economic cultural context in a developing society. In the shadow of economic growth, cultural boons are disvalued. Cooking for granny is redefined as work in the employ of the household whose contribution to the economy can be measured by one of many methods. Or it is discussed as an undesirable remnant of the past, which ought to be eliminated through further development. In both perspectives, giving grandmother her due has been turned into a disvalue once the activity — in this case, cooking late breakfast — is construed as a value which is produced to satisfy her needs.

Economic value arises and overshadows blessings when and where the cultural context is laid waste. The creation of disvalue is the logical precondition for the appearance of economic concepts and the experiences these concepts induce.

I here choose the term 'disvalue' for the same reasons for which, earlier, I chose blessings. With these terms I want to designate respectively loss and boon of a kind that cannot be gauged in economic terms. The economist can price a loss. He can calculate external costs, that is, those losses to others that are caused by a product, and that can be internalized into its price. He can calculate depreciation and risks. He can measure the losses caused by obsolescence. For example, he can calculate the amount of damage that has been caused to millions of clients by the recent switch of IBM to a new model. But with concepts that formalize choices under the assumption of scarcity, he has no means to gauge the experience of a person who loses the effective use of his feet because vehicles have established a radical monopoly over locomotion. What that person is deprived of is not in the domain of scarcity. Now, to get from here to there, that person must purchase passenger miles. The geographic environment now blocks his feet. Space has been turned into an infrastructure for vehicles. It would be misleading to call this the obsolescence of feet. Feet are not 'rudimentary means of self transportation', as some traffic engineers would have it. However, since most people are by now 'economized' (a condition perhaps similar to being anesthetized), they are blind and indifferent to the loss induced by what I call disvalue.

My meaning becomes more clear when disvalue is contrasted with waste. The latter once meant the abuse that deprives a fertile tract of land of its fruitfulness, in the same way that human geography is now deprived by vehicular traffic of its proportionality to feet. But this is not what waste now means. Since about 1840, waste has meant a new kind of stuff, of which I find no evidence in earlier sources. Peasant societies and earlier towns knew no waste. Even at the onset of industrial production, waste still meant what falls off the workbench. It then comes to be recognized as a stuff produced by industry that is a 'no-good' to such a degree that it must be removed at almost any cost. Waste, therefore, became an eminently economic category. It could be used as a measure to recognize when disutilities outgrew utilities. But both these economic terms, utilities and disutilities, acquire their respective values to the degree that the matrix that engenders blessings is being destroyed, that is, disvalued. People only then become dependent on motorized crutches when their feet have been crippled by a new environment.

In this new environment, people can no longer avoid transportation. But even worse: the belief arises that in comparison to an accessible world this new environment is a greater good. Indirectly, good of a lower kind is attributed to a pedestrian world. As a consequence, a decline in transportation is seen as a loss.

I am here to plead among economists for help in establishing a discourse in which — being careful not to reduce these substantively non-economic experiences to economic terms — a decline in economic production raises a new question: is this a condition for the recovery of blessings? In such a discourse the key issue is the limitation of economics, and especially the removal of the shadow thrown by economic structures onto the cultural domain. For this purpose we need to learn how to speak in a disciplined way about public issues, choosing words that do not surreptitiously drag in assumptions of scarcity. Only insofar as values come to be recognized in their subsidiary relationship to what I call 'blessings' am I able to speak in a disciplined way about public life after the crash of development. When that happens, we can speak about the renunciation of values as a condition for the good life.

Silence is a Commons

Opening remarks at the
'Asahi Symposium: Science and Man —
The Computer-Managed Society'
Tokyo, 21st March 1982

Minna-san, gladly I accept the honor of addressing this forum on Science and Man. The theme that Mr Tsuru proposes, 'The Computer-Managed Society,' sounds an alarm. Clearly you foresee that machines which ape people are tending to encroach on every aspect of people's lives, and that such machines force people to behave like machines. The new electronic devices do indeed have the power to force people to 'communicate' with them and with each other on the terms of the machine. Whatever structurally does not fit the logic of machines is effectively filtered from a culture dominated by their use.

The machine-like behavior of people chained to electronics constitutes a degradation of their well-being and of their dignity which, for most people in the long run, becomes intolerable. Observations of the sickening effect of programmed environments show that people in them become indolent, impotent, narcissistic and apolitical. The political process breaks down because people cease to be able to govern themselves; they demand to be managed.

I congratulate Asahi Shimbun on its efforts to foster a new democratic consensus in Japan, by which your more than seven million readers become aware of the need to limit the encroachment of machines on the style of their own behavior. It is important that it is precisely Japan that initiates such action. Japan is looked upon as the capital of electronics; it would be marvelous if it became for the entire world the model of a new politics of self-limitation in the field of communication which, in my opinion, is henceforth necessary if a people wants to remain self-governing.

Electronic management as a political issue can be approached in several ways. I propose, at the beginning of this public consultation, to approach the issue as one of political ecology. Ecology, during the last ten years, has acquired a new meaning. It is still the name for a branch of professional biology, but the term now increasingly serves as the label under which a broad, politically organized general public analyzes and influences technical decisions. I want to focus on the new electronic management devices as a technical change of the human environment which, to be benign, must remain under political (and not exclusively expert) control. I have chosen this focus for my conversation with those three Japanese colleagues to whom I owe what I know about your country — Professors Yoshikazu Sakamoto, Joshiro Tamanoi and Jun Ui.

In the thirteen minutes still left to me on this rostrum I will clarify a distinction that I consider fundamental to political ecology. I shall distinguish the environment as commons from the environment as resource. On our ability to make this particular distinction depends not only the construction of a sound theoretical ecology, but also — and more importantly — effective ecological jurisprudence.

Minna-san, how I wish, at this point, that I were a pupil trained by your Zen poet, the great Basho. Then perhaps in a bare seventeen syllables I could express the distinction between the commons within which people's subsistence activities are embedded, and resources that serve for the economic production of those commodities on which modern survival depends. If I were a poet, perhaps I would make this distinction so beautifully and incisively that it would penetrate your hearts and remain unforgettable. Unfortunately I am not a Japanese poet. I must speak to you in English, a language that during the last hundred years has lost the ability to make this distinction, and — in addition —

I must speak through translation. Only because I may count on the translating genius of Mr Muramatsu do I dare to recover old English meanings with a talk in Japan.

'Commons' is a Middle English word. According to my Japanese friends, it is quite close to the meaning that *iriai* still has in Japanese. 'Commons,' like *iriai*, is a word which, in pre-industrial times, was used to designate certain aspects of the environment. People called commons those parts of the environment for which customary law exacted specific forms of community respect. People called commons that part of the environment which lay beyond their own thresholds and outside of their own possessions, to which, however, they had recognized claims of usage, not to produce commodities but to provide for the subsistence of their households. The customary law which humanized the environment by establishing the commons was usually unwritten. It was unwritten law not only because people did not care to write it down, but because what it protected was a reality much too complex to fit into paragraphs. The law of the commons regulates the right of way, the right to fish and to hunt, to graze, and to collect wood or medicinal plants in the forest.

An oak tree might be in the commons. Its shade, in summer, is reserved for the shepherd and his flock; its acorns are reserved for the pigs of the neighboring peasants; its dry branches serve as fuel for the widows of the village; some of its fresh twigs in springtime are cut as ornaments for the church — and at sunset it might be the place for the village assembly. When people spoke about commons, *iriai*, they designated an aspect of the environment that was limited, that was necessary for the community's survival, that was necessary for different groups in different ways, but which, in a strictly economic sense, was not perceived as scarce.

When I am in Europe with university students today, I use the term 'commons' (in German *Allmende* or *Gemeinheit*; in Italian *gli usi civici*), and my listeners immediately think of the eighteenth century. They think of those pastures in England on which each villager kept a few sheep, and they think of the 'enclosure of the pastures' which transformed the grassland from commons into a resource on which commercial flocks could be raised. Primarily, however, my students think of the innovation of poverty which came with enclosure: of the absolute impoverishment of the peasants who were driven from the land and into wage-labor, and they think of the commercial enrichment of the lords.

In their immediate reaction, my students think of the rise of a new capitalist order. Facing that painful newness, they forget that enclosure also stands for something more basic. The enclosure of the commons inaugurates a new ecological order. Enclosure did not just physically transfer the control over grasslands from the peasants to the lord. It marked a radical change in the attitudes of society toward the environment. Before, in any juridical system, most of the environment had been considered as commons from which most people could draw most of their sustenance without needing to take recourse to the market. After enclosure the environment became primarily a resource at the service of 'enterprises' which, by organizing wage-labor, transformed nature into the goods and services on which the satisfaction of basic needs by consumers depends. This transformation is the blind spot of political economy.

This change of attitudes can be illustrated better if we think about roads rather than about grasslands. What a difference there was between the new and the old parts of Mexico City only 20 years ago. In the old parts of the city the streets were true commons. Some people sat on the road to sell vegetables and charcoal. Others put their chairs on the road to drink coffee or tequila. Others held their meetings on the road to decide on the new headman for the neighborhood or to determine the price of a donkey. Others drove their donkeys through the crowd, walking next to the heavily-laden beast of burden; others sat in the saddle. Children played in the gutter, and people walking could still use the road to get from one place to another.

Such roads were built for people. Like any true commons, the street itself was the result of people living there and making that space livable. The dwellings that lined the roads were not private homes in the modern sense — garages for the overnight deposit of workers. The threshold still separated two living spaces, one intimate and one common. But neither homes in this intimate sense nor streets as commons survived economic development.

In the new sections of Mexico City, streets are no longer for people. They are now roadways for automobiles, for buses, for taxis, cars, and trucks. People are barely tolerated on the streets unless they are on their way to a bus stop. If people now sat down or stopped on the street, they would become obstacles for traffic, and the traffic would be dangerous to them. The road has been degraded from a commons to a simple resource for the circulation of vehicles. People can circulate no more on their own. Traffic has displaced their mobility. They can circulate only when they are strapped down and are moved.

The appropriation of the grassland by the lords was challenged, but the more fundamental transformation of grassland (or of roads) from commons to resource has happened, until recently, without being subjected to criticism. The appropriation of the environment by the few was clearly recognized as an intolerable abuse. By contrast, the even more degrading transformation of people into members of an industrial labor force and into consumers was, until recently, taken for granted. For almost a hundred years many political parties have challenged the accumulation of environmental resources in private hands. However, the issue was argued in terms of the private utilization of these resources, not the extinction of commons. Thus anticapitalist politics so far have bolstered the legitimacy of transforming commons into resources.

Only recently, at the base of society, a new kind of 'popular intellectual' is beginning to recognize what has been happening. Enclosure has denied the people the right to that kind of environment on which — throughout all of history — the moral economy of survival depends. Enclosure, once accepted, redefines community. Enclosure undermines the local autonomy of community. Enclosure of the commons is thus as much in the interest of professionals and of state bureaucrats as it is in the interest of capitalists.

Enclosure allows the bureaucrat to define local community as impotent to provide for its own survival. People become economic individuals who depend for their survival on commodities that are produced for them. Fundamentally, most citizens' movements represent a rebellion against this environmentally-induced redefinition of people as consumers.

Minna-san, you wanted to hear me speak on electronics, not grassland and roads. But I am a historian; I wanted to speak first about the pastoral commons as I know them from the past in order then to say something about the present much wider threat to the commons by electronics.

This man who speaks to you was born 55 years ago in Vienna. One month after his birth he was put on a train, and then on a ship and brought to the Island of Brac. Here, in a village on the Dalmatian coast, his grandfather wanted to bless him. My grandfather lived in the house in which his family had lived since the time when Muromachi ruled in Kyoto. Since then on the Dalmatian Coast many rulers had come and gone — the doges of Venice, the sultans of Istanbul, the corsairs of Almissa, the emperors of Austria, and the kings of Yugoslavia. But the many changes in the uniform and language of the governors had altered little in daily life during those 500 years. The very same olive-wood rafters still supported the roof of my grandfather's house. Water was still gathered from the same stone slabs on the roof. The wine was pressed in the same vats, the fish caught from the same kind of boat, and the oil came from trees planted when Edo was in its youth.

My grandfather had received news twice a month. The news now arrived by steamer in three days; formerly, by sloop, it had taken five days to arrive. When I was born, for the people who lived off the main routes, history still flowed slowly, imperceptibly. Most of the environment was in the commons. People lived in houses they had built; moved on streets that had been trampled by the feet of their animals; were autonomous in the procurement and disposal of their water; could depend on their own voices when they wanted to speak up. All this changed with my arrival in Brac.

On the same boat on which I arrived in 1926, the first loudspeaker was landed on the island. Few people there had ever heard of such a thing. Up to that day, all men and women had spoken with more or less equally powerful voices. Henceforth this would change. Henceforth the access to the microphone would determine whose voice shall be magnified. Silence now ceased to be in the commons; it became a resource for which loudspeakers compete. Language itself was transformed thereby from a local commons into a national resource for communication. As enclosure by the lords increased national productivity by denying the individual peasant to keep a few sheep, so the encroachment of the loudspeaker destroyed that silence which so far had given each man and woman his or her proper and equal voice. Unless you have access to a loudspeaker, you are silenced.

I hope that the parallel now becomes clear. Just as the commons of space are vulnerable and can be destroyed by the motorization of traffic, so the commons of speech are vulnerable and can easily be destroyed by the encroachment of modern means of communication.

The issue which I propose for discussion should therefore be clear: how to counter the encroachment of new, electronic devices and systems upon commons that are more subtle and more intimate to our being than either grassland or roads — commons that are at least as valuable as silence. Silence, according to Western and Eastern tradition alike, is necessary for the emergence of persons. It is taken from us by machines that ape people. We could easily be made increasingly dependent on machines for speaking and for thinking, as we are already dependent on machines for moving.

Such a transformation of the environment from a commons to a productive resource constitutes the most fundamental form of environmental degradation. This degradation has a long history, which coincides with the history of capitalism but can in no way just be reduced to it. Unfortunately, the importance of this transformation has been overlooked or belittled by political ecology so far. It needs to be recognized if we are to organize defense movements for what remains of the commons. This defense constitutes the crucial public task for political action during the eighties. The task must be undertaken urgently because commons can exist without police, but resources cannot. Just as traffic, computers call for police, and for ever more of them, and in ever more subtle forms.

By definition, resources call for defense by police. Once they are defended, their recovery as commons becomes increasingly difficult. This is a special reason for urgency.

Dwelling

Address to the Royal Institute of British Architects
York, U.K., July 1984.
(Celebration of the 150th anniversary of
the Royal Institute of British Architects)

To dwell is human. Wild beasts have nests, cattle have stables, carriages fit into sheds, and there are garages for automobiles. Only humans can dwell. To dwell is an art. Every spider is born with a compulsion to weave a web particular to its kind. Spiders, like all animals, are programmed by their genes. The human is the only animal who is an artist, and the art of dwelling is part of the art of living. A house is neither nest nor garage.

Most languages use living in the sense of dwelling. To put the question, 'where do you live?' is to ask for the place where your daily existence gives shape to the world. Just tell me how you dwell and I will tell you who you are. This equation of dwelling and living goes back to times when the world was still habitable and humans were in-habitants. To dwell then meant to inhabit one's own traces, to let daily life write the webs and knots of one's biography into the landscape. This writing could be etched into stone by successive generations or sketched anew for each rainy season with a few reeds and leaves. Man's habitable traces were as ephemeral as their inhabitants. Dwellings were never completed before occupancy, in contrast to the contemporary commodity, which decays from the day it is ready to use. A tent had to be mended daily, it had to be put up, stretched, pulled down. A homestead waxes and wanes with the state of its members: you can often discern from a distant slope whether the children are married, whether the old ones have already died. Building goes on from lifetime to lifetime; rituals mark its prominent stages: generations might have passed since the laying of the cornerstone until the cutting of the rafters. Nor is the quarter of a town ever completed; right into the eighteenth century the residents of popular quarters defended their own art of dwelling by rioting against the improvements that architects tried to foist on them. Dwelling is part of that moral economy which E.P. Thompson has so well described. It succumbed to the king's avenues, which in the name of order, cleanliness, security and decorum tore up the neighborhoods. It succumbed to the police which in the nineteenth century named streets and numbered houses. It succumbed to the professionals who introduced sewers and controls. It was almost extinguished by welfare, which exalted the right of each citizen to his own garage and TV.

Dwelling is an activity that lies beyond the reach of the architect not only because it is a popular art; not only because it goes on and on in waves that escape his control; not only because it is of a tender complexity outside of the horizon of mere biologists and system analysts; but above all because no two communities dwell alike. Habit and habitat say almost the same. Each vernacular architecture (to use the anthropologist's term) is as unique as vernacular speech. The art of living in its entirety — that is, the art of loving and dreaming, of suffering and dying — makes each lifestyle unique. And therefore this art is much too complex to be taught by the methods of a Comenius or Pestalozzi, by a schoolmaster or by TV. It is an art which can only be picked up. Each person becomes a vernacular builder and a vernacular speaker by growing up, by moving from one initiation to the next in becoming either a male or a female inhabitant. Therefore the Cartesian, three-dimensional, homogeneous space into which the architect builds, and the vernacular space which dwelling brings into existence, constitute different classes of space. Architects can do nothing but build. Vernacular dwellers generate the axioms of the spaces they inhabit.

The contemporary consumer of residence space lives topologically in another world. The coordinates of residential space within which he locates himself are the only world of which he has had experience. He finds it impossible to believe that the cattle-herding Peul and the cliff-hanging Dogon and the fishing Songhai and the tilling Bobo live in heterogeneous spaces that fit into the very same landscape, as seen by most ecologists. For the modern resident a mile is a mile, and after each mile comes another, because the world has no center. For the dweller the center of the world is the place where he lives, and ten miles up the river might be much closer than one mile into the desert. According to many anthropologists, the dweller's culture distorts his vision. In fact, it determines the characteristics of the space he inhabits.

The resident has lost much of his power to dwell. The necessity to sleep under a roof for him has been transmogrified into a culturally defined need. The liberty to dwell has become insignificant for him. He needs the right to claim a certain number of square feet in built-up space. He treasures entitlements to deliveries and the skills to use them. The art of living for him is forfeited: he has no need for the art of dwelling because he needs an apartment; just as he has no need for the art of suffering because he counts on medical assistance and has probably never thought about the art of dying.

The resident lives in a world that has been made. He can no more beat his path on the highway than he can make a hole in a wall. He goes through life without leaving a trace. The marks he leaves are considered dents — wear and tear. What he does leave behind him will be removed as garbage. From commons for dwelling the environment has been redefined as a resource for the production of garages for people, commodities and cars. Housing provides cubicles in which residents are housed. Such housing is planned, built and equipped for them. To be allowed to dwell minimally in one's own housing constitutes a special privilege: only the rich may move a door or drive a nail into a wall. Thus the vernacular space of dwelling is replaced by the homogeneous space of the garage. Settlements look the same from Taiwan to Ohio and from Lima to Peking. Everywhere you find the same garage for the human — shelves to store the work-force overnight, handy for the means of its transportation. Inhabitants dwelling in spaces they fashion have been replaced by residents sheltered in buildings produced for them, duly registered as consumers of housing protected by the Tenants' or the Credit Receivers' Act.

To be put up in most societies is a sign of misery: the orphan is taken in, the pilgrim put up, the condemned man imprisoned, the slave locked up overnight and the soldier — but only since the eighteenth century — billeted in barracks. Before that even the army had to provide its own dwelling by camping. Industrial society is the only one which attempts to make every citizen into a resident who must be sheltered and thus is absolved from the duty of that social and communitary activity that I call dwelling. Those who insist now on their liberty to dwell on their own are either very well off or treated as deviants. This is true both for those whom so-called 'development' has not yet untaught the desire to dwell, and for the unpluggers who seek new forms of dwelling that would make the industrial landscape inhabitable — at least in its cracks and weak spots.

Both the non-modernized and the post-modern oppose society's ban on spatial self-assertion, and will have to reckon with the police intervening against the nuisance they create. They will be branded as intruders, illegal occupants, anarchists and nuisances, depending on the circumstance under which they assert their liberty to dwell: as Indians who break in and settle on fallow land in Lima; as *favellados* in Rio de Janeiro, who return to squat on the hillside from which they have just been driven — after 40 years' occupancy — by the police; as students who dare to convert ruins in Berlin's Kreuzberg into their dwelling; as Puerto Ricans who force their way back into the walled-up and burnt buildings of the South Bronx. They will all be removed, not so much because of the damage they do to the owner of the site, or because they threaten the health or peace of their neighbors, but because of the challenge to the social axiom that defines a citizen as a unit in need of a standard garage.

Both the Indian tribe that moves down from the Andes into the suburbs of Lima and the Chicago neighborhood council that unplugs itself from the city housing authority challenge the now-prevalent model of the citizen as *homo castrensis*, billeted man. But with their challenges, the newcomer and the breakaway provoke opposite reactions. The Indios can be treated like pagans who must be educated into an appreciation of the state's maternal care for their shelter. The unplugger is much more dangerous: he gives testimony to the castrating effects of the city's maternal embrace. Unlike the pagan, this kind of heretic challenges the axiom of civic religion which underlies all current ideologies which on the surface are in opposition. According to this axiom, the citizen as *homo castrensis* needs the commodity called 'shelter'; his right to shelter is written into the law. This right the unplugger does not oppose, but he does object to the concrete conditions under which the right to shelter is in conflict with the liberty to dwell. And for the unplugger this liberty, when in conflict, is presumed to be of greater value than the commodity of shelter, which by definition is scarce.

The conflict between vernacular and economic values is, however, not limited to the space on the inside of the threshold. It would be a mistake to limit the effects of dwelling to the shaping of the interiors; what lies outside one's front door is as much shaped by dwelling, albeit in a different way. Inhabited land lies on both sides of the threshold; the threshold is like the pivot of the space that dwelling creates. On this side lies home, and on the other lies the commons: the space that households inhabit is common. It shelters the community as the house shelters its members. Just as no two communities have the same style of dwelling, none can have the same commons. Custom rules who may and who must use the commons, and how and when and where. Just as the home reflects in its shape the rhythm and extent of family life, so the commons are the trace of the commonality. There can be no dwelling without its commons. It takes time for the immigrant to recognize that highways are neither streets nor paths but resources reserved for transportation. I have seen many Puerto Ricans who arrived in New York and needed years to discover that sidewalks were not part of a plaza. All over Europe, to the despair of German bureaucrats, Turks pull their chairs into the street for a chat, for a bet, for some business, to be served coffee and to put up a stall. It takes time to forego the commons, to recognize that traffic is as lethal to business as to gossip outside the doorway. The distinction between private and public space for the modern shelter consumer does not replace but destroys the traditional distinction between the home and the commons articulated by the threshold. However, what housing as a commodity has done to the environment has so far not been recognized by our ecologists. Ecology still acts as a subsidiary or twin to economics. Political ecology will become radical and effective only as it recognizes that the destruction of the commons by their transformation into economic resources is the environmental factor which paralyzes the art of dwelling.

One demonstration of the destruction of commons is the degree to which our world has become uninhabitable. As the number of people increases, paradoxically we render the environment uninhabitable. Just as more people need to dwell, the war against vernacular dwelling has entered its last stage and people are forced to seek housing which is scarce. A generation ago Jane Jacobs effectively argued that in traditional cities the art of dwelling and the aliveness of the commons increase both as cities expand and also as people move closer together. And yet during the last thirty years almost everywhere in the world, powerful means have been employed to rape the local community's art of dwelling and thereby create an increasingly acute sense of scarce living space.

This housing rape of the commons is no less brutal than the poisoning of water. The invasion of the last enclaves of dwelling space by housing programs is no less obnoxious than the creation of smog. The ever-repeated juristic prejudice in favor of the right to housing, whenever this claim conflicts with the liberty to explore new ways of dwelling, is as repressive as the laws which enforce the lifestyle of the 'productive human' couple. However, it needs to be pro-claimed. Air, water and alternative ways of cohabitation have found their protectors. Curricula offer them training, and bureaucracies offer them jobs. The liberty to dwell and the protection of a habitable environment for the moment remain the concern of minority citizens' movements; and even these movements are all too often corrupted by archi-tects who misinterpret their aims.

'Build-it-yourself' is thought of as a mere hobby — or as a consolation for shanty-towns. The return to rural life is dubbed romanticism. Inner-city fishponds and chickencoops are regarded as mere games. Neighborhoods that 'work' are flooded by highly-paid sociologists until they fail. House-squatting is regarded as civil disobedience, restorative squat-ting as an outcry for better and more housing. But in the field of housing, as much as in the fields of education, medicine, transportation or burial, those who unplug themselves are no purists. I know a family that herds a few goats in the Appalachians and in the evening plays with a battery-powered computer. I know an illegal occupant who has broken into a walled-up Harlem tenement and sends his daughters to a private school.

Yet neither ridicule nor psychiatric diagnosis will make the unpluggers go away. They have lost the conscience of the Calvinist hippies and grow their own brand of sarcasm and political skill. Their own experience tells them that they enjoy the art of living which they recover by dwelling more than they enjoyed the comfort they left. And increasingly they become more capable of putting into pithy gestures their rejection of the axioms about *homo castrensis* on which industrial society partly rests.

And there are other considerations which make the recov-ery of dwelling space seem reasonable today. Modern meth-ods, materials and machines make build-it-yourself ever so much simpler and less tiresome than it was before. Growing unemployment takes the stigma of being asocial away from those who short-circuit the building unions. Increasingly, trained construction workers have to relearn completely their trade to ply it in a form of unemployment which is useful to them and their community. The gross inefficiency of buildings put up in the seventies makes previously unthinkable transformations seem less odious, and even reasonable, to neighbors who would have protested a few years ago. The experience of the Third World converges with the experience in the South Bronx. The president of Mexico, while campaigning for election, stated without ambiguity: the Mexican economy cannot now nor in the future provide housing units for most of its citizens. The only way in which all Mexicans will be agreeably housed will be via provision in laws and of materials that enable each Mexican community to house itself better than ever before.

What is here proposed is enormous: the unplugging of a nation from the worldwide market in housing units. I do not believe that a Third World country can do this. As long as a country considers itself underdeveloped, it takes its models from the North, be this the capitalist or the socialist cheek. I cannot believe that such a country could really unplug itself, as a nation. Too much power accrues to any government from the ideology of man 'billeted' by nature. The utopia of nation building and housing construction are closely linked in the thinking of all élites I know, especially in the Third World. I believe that liberty to dwell, and the provision of the instruments — legal and material — to make this choice feasible, must be recognized first in the countries that are 'developed.' Here the unplugger can argue with much more conviction and precision why he places this liberty above the entitlement to a garage. Let him then look to Mexico to learn what adobe can do.

And the arguments that place the recovery of vernacular power to dwell over the impotent claims to personal storage are on the increase. As we have seen, they are consistent with the direction the ecological movement takes when it does get out from under the wings of the economy, the science of scarce values. They are consistent with a new radical analysis of technology that opposes the enrolment of people as volunteers in the building industry and modern tools adopted by people to remedy their defective ability to dwell. But more important than these is the argument that has not yet been properly formulated, but that I read into many of the concrete initiatives that I have observed.

Space fit to bear the marks of life is as basic for suvival as clean water and fresh air. Human beings simply do not fit into garages, no matter how splendidly furnished with showers and energy-saving devices. Homes and garages are just not the same sort of space. Homes are neither the human nests to which sociobiologists would reduce them, nor shelves on which people cannot survive regardless of how well they are cushioned. Garages are storage spaces for objects that circulate through the homogeneous space of commodities; nests are shaped and occupied by animals whose instincts tie them to their territory. Humans dwell. They have inhabited the Earth in a thousand different ways and copied from each other the forms of their dwellings. What had determined for millenia the changing character of the dwelling space was not instinct and genes but culture, experience and thought. Both territory and dwelling space are, admittedly, three-dimensional in character, but as to their meaning, they are not spaces of the same kind — no more than dwelling space and garages. None of the sciences that we now have can properly grasp this variety of topologies — neither sociology, nor anthropology, nor can history as now mostly undertaken abandon the central perspective in which the differences that count disappear. I do believe that the disciplined opposition of human experience under the reign of vernacular values, and under the regime of scarcity, is a first step toward clarifying this difference — which counts. And without the recovery of a language in which this difference can be stated, the refusal to identify with the model of 'billeted man' and the search for new vernacular dwelling space cannot become politically effective. .

And so, when the act of dwelling becomes a subject of politics, it comes inevitably to a parting of the ways. On the one side there will be concern for the 'housing package' — how to entitle everyone to get their share of built cubage, well situated and well equipped. On this side the packaging of the poor with their housing unit will become a growth sector for social workers when there is no more money left for the architects. On the other side there will be concern for the right of a community to form and accommodate itself according to its ability and art. In the pursuit of this goal it will appear to many in the North that the fragmenting of the habitat and the loss of traditions has caused the right to a dwellable habitat to be forfeited. Young people who insist on housing themselves will look with envy Southwards, where space and tradition are still alive.

This budding envy of the underdeveloped must be cured with courage and reflection. But in the Third World survival itself depends on the correct balance between a right to 'build-it-yourself' and the right to possess a piece of land and some things such as one's own roof rafters.

The Message of Bapu's Hut

Inaugural Speech
Sevagram Ashram Pratishthan
Sevagram, Wardha. January 1978

This morning, while I was sitting in this hut where Mahatma Gandhi lived, I was trying to absorb the spirit of its concept and imbibe in me its message. There are two things about the hut which have impressed me greatly. One is its spiritual aspect and the other is the aspect of its amenities. I was trying to understand Gandhi's point of view in regard to making the hut. I very much liked its simplicity, beauty and neatness. The hut proclaims the principle of love and equality with everybody. Since the house which has been provided for me in Mexico is in many ways like this hut, I could understand its spirit. Here I found that the hut has seven kinds of place. As you enter, there is a place where you put down your shoes and prepare yourself physically and mentally to go into the hut. Then comes the central room which is big enough to accommodate a large family. Today, at four in the morning, when I was sitting there for prayer, four people sat along with me, by supporting themselves on one wall, and on the other side there was also enough room for as many people again, if they sat close together. This room is where everybody can go and join others. The third space is where Gandhi himself sat and worked. There are two more rooms — one for the guests and the other for the sick. There is an open verandah and also a commodious bathroom. All of these places have a very organic relationship.

I feel that if rich people come to this hut, they might be making fun of it. But from the point of view of a simple Indian, I do not see why there should be a house bigger than this. This house is made of wood and mud. In its making, it is not the machine, but the hands of man which have worked. I call it a hut, but it is really a home. There is a difference between a house and a home. A house is where man keeps his luggage and furniture. It is meant more for the security and convenience of the furniture than of the man himself. In Delhi, where I had been put up, is a house where there are many conveniences. The building is constructed from the point of view of these conveniences. It is made of cement and bricks and is like a box where the furniture and other conveniences can fit in well. We must understand that all furniture and other articles that we go on collecting in our lives will never give us inner strength. These are, so to say, the crutches of a cripple. The more of such conveniences we have, the more our dependence on them increases and our life gets restricted. On the contrary, the kind of furniture I find in Gandhi's hut is of a different order, and there is very little cause for being dependent on it. A house fitted with all kinds of conveniences shows that we have become weak. The more we lose the power to live, the greater we depend upon the goods we acquire. It is like our depending upon hospitals for the health of people and upon schools for the education of our children. Unfortunately, both hospitals and schools are not an index of the health or the intelligence of a nation. Actually, the number of hospitals is indicative of the ill health of people and schools of their ignorance. Similarly, the multiplicity of facilities in living minimizes the expression of creativity in human life.

Unfortunately, the paradox of the situation is that those who have more such conveniences are regarded as superior. Is it not an immoral society where illness is accorded high status and ignorance more consideration? While sitting in Gandhi's hut I was grieved to ponder over this perversity. I have come to the conclusion that it is wrong to think of industrial civilization as a road leading toward the development of man. It has been proved that for our economic development, greater and bigger machines of production and larger and larger numbers of engineers, doctors and professors are literally supernumery.

Those who would want to have a place bigger than this hut where Gandhi lived are poor in mind, body and life style. I pity them. They have surrendered themselves and their animate selves to an inanimate structure. In the process they have lost the elasticity of their body and the vitality of their life. They have little relationship with nature and closeness with their fellowmen.

When I ask the planners of the day why they do not understand the simple approach Gandhi taught us, they say that Gandhi's way is very difficult, and that people will not be able to follow it. But the reality of the situation is that since Gandhi's principles do not tolerate the presence of any middleman or that of a centralized system, the planners and managers and politicians feel left out. How is it that such a simple principle of truth and non-violence is not being understood? Is it because people feel that untruth and violence will take them to the desired objective? No. This is not so. The common man fully understands that right means will take him to the right end. It is only the people who have some vested interest who refuse to understand it. The rich do not want to understand. By 'rich' I mean those who have conveniences of life which are not available to everybody in common. There are the 'rich' in living, eating, and getting about; and their modes of consumption are such that they have been blinded to truth. It is to the blind that Gandhi becomes a difficult proposition to understand and assimilate. They are the ones to whom simplicity does not make any sense. Their circumstances unfortunately do not allow them to see the truth. Their lives have become too complicated to enable them to get out of the trap they are in. Fortunately, for the largest number of people, there is neither so much of wealth that they become immune to the truth of simplicity, nor are they in such penury that they lack the capacity to understand. Even if the rich see the truth they refuse to abide by it. It is because they have lost contact with the soul of this country.

It should be very clear that the dignity of man is possible only in a self-sufficient society and that it suffers as one moves toward progressive industrialization. This hut connotes the pleasures that are possible through being at par with society. Here, self-sufficiency is the keynote. We must understand that the unnecessary articles and goods which a man possesses reduce his power to imbibe happiness from the surroundings. Therefore, Gandhi repeatedly said that productivity should be kept within the limits of wants. Today's mode of production is such that it finds no limit and goes on increasing, uninhibited. All these we have been tolerating so far, but the time has come when man must understand that by depending more and more on machines he is moving toward his own destruction. The civilized world, whether it is China or America, has begun to understand that if we want to progress, this is not the way. Man should realize that for the good of the individual as well as of society, it is best that people keep for themselves only as much as is sufficient for their immediate needs. We have to find a method by which this thinking finds expression in changing the values of today's world. This change cannot be brought about by the pressure of governments or through centralized institutions. A climate of public opinion has to be created to make people understand that which constitutes the basic society. Today the man with a motor car thinks himself superior to the man with a bicycle, though when we look at it from the point of view of the common norm, it is the bicycle which is the vehicle of the masses. The cycle, therefore, must be given the prime importance and all the planning in roads and transport should be done on the basis of the bicycle, whereas the motor car should get secondary place. The situation, however, is the reverse and all plans are made for the benefit of the motor car giving second place to the bicycle. Common man's requirements are thus disregarded in comparison with those of the higher-ups. This hut of Gandhi's demonstrates to the world how the dignity of the common man can be brought up. It is also a symbol of the happiness that we can derive from practising the principles of simplicity, service and truthfulness. I hope that in the

conference that you are going to hold on Techniques for the
Third World Poor, you will try to keep this message before
you.

Disvalue

Lecture to the first public meeting of the Entropy Society
Tokyo, Keyo University, 9th November 1986
Enlarged and combined with
'Disvaluation: The Secret Capital Accumulation'
and 'Beauty and the Junkyard'
two unpublished manuscripts completed in March 1987

Professor Tamanoy's Forum

This first public meeting of the Japanese Entropy Society provides us with an occasion to commemorate Professor Joshiro Tamanoy. Most of us knew him as friends and as pupils. The questions he asked bring together today 600 physicists and biologists, economists and green activists.

While a Professor of Economics at Tokyo University, he translated Karl Polanyi into Japanese. But in his own teaching and writing he brought a uniquely Japanese flavor to ecological research by relating cultural to physical dimensions. He did so by focusing on the interaction between an epoch's economic ideology and the corresponding soil-water matrix of social life. He was an active environmental politician and a master teacher. And no one who experienced his friendship will ever forget its delicacy.

How to name an evil

He had few illusions. Courageously he reflected on the causes of modern war, modern ugliness and modern social inequity to the point of facing almost unbearable horror. But no one will forget Tamanoy-sensei's balance. He never lost his compassion and subtle humor. He introduced me to the world of those who survived with the marks of the Hiroshima bomb, the *hibakusha*. And I think of him as a spiritual *hibakusha*. He lived the 'examined life' in the shadow of Hiroshima and Minamata. Under this cloud he forged a terminology to relate historical spaces to physical place. To this purpose he used 'entropy' as a *semeion*, a signal for the impending threat to an exquisitely Japanese perception of locality referred to with terms which seem to have no comparable Western equivalent, like *fûdô*. And entropy was central to our conversations. In this lecture I want to explore the limits within which the notion of entropy can be usefully applied to social phenomena by comparing it to the notion of waste. I will then propose the notion of 'disvalue' in the hope that through it entropy, when used outside of physics and information theory, will be more clearly understood.

Clausius, a German physicist, first introduced the word. In 1850 he studied the ratio between the heat content and the absolute pressure in a closed system and felt the need for a word to name this function. He was an amateur classicist and picked the Greek word *entropy* in 1865. Since then it is used for the algorithm that describes a previously unrecognized phenomenon. By choosing *this* word, Clausius did us a favor. *Entrópeo* in classical Greek means to turn, to twist, to pervert or to humiliate. More than a century after its introduction in physics, the Greek word still seems able to bespeak a previously unknown frustrating twist that perverts our best social energies and moral intentions.

In a few years the word has become a catchall for a variety of paradoxical twists which have two things in common. They are so new that everyday language has no traditional defined meaning for them and are so maddening that people are happy to avoid mentioning them. To taboo their own implication in non-sustainable consumption of goods and services, people grab at the non-word 'entropy' to make social degradation appear as just another instance of a general natural law.

When people discuss the cultural impoverishment that appears in stupefying schooling, sickening medicine and time-killing acceleration, they are talking about perversions of good intentions, not about instances of energy or information flow. They mean the evil effects of untoward social goals that have none of the innocence of the inexorable determinism we associate with entropy in physics. The degradation of cultural variety through transnational organization of money flow is a result of greed, not a law of nature. The disappearance of subsistence cultures tied to local soils is a historical and dramatic part of the human condition *only* in recent times. The disappearance of 'ideologies' that favor the water-soil matrix is due to human enterprise and endeavor. What late twentieth-century people take for granted is not something which has always been.

Tamanoy made me understand that it is possible to include soil, water and sun in philosophical anthropology, to speak of a 'philosophy of soil.' After my conversations with him I rediscovered Paracelsus, who calls for the same approach. A philosophy of soil starts from the certainty that reason is worthless without a reciprocal shaping of norms and tangible reality; *seeing* the culturally shaped body cum 'environment' as it is in a concrete place and time. And this interaction is formed by esthetic and moral style as much as by the 'spirits' which ritual and art evoke from the earthly matrix of a place. The disappearance of corresponding matrices of soil and society is an issue which we cannot examine deeply enough. And for this, comparison between the *wasting* of cultural variety and the cosmic degradation of energy can be useful, but only under one condition: that we clearly understand the limits within which science can still generate metaphors. As a metaphor, entropy can be an eye opener. As an explanatory analog it cannot but mystify.

*Entropy as a metaphor versus
entropy as a reductive analog*

My last conversation with Dr Tamanoy took place after a

long tour of his native island. He took me around Okinawa
to meet with his friends, to battlefields, cave-refuges and
refineries. From a curve on a mountain road we looked at the
Japanese oil reserves and the bay which now lay waste. The
shellfish, gardens and village life were gone. Our conversation turned to the danger of extrapolating from a dying tree
to global pollution. No doubt, the latter evil is world-wide.
But such world-wide despoliation and its tangible evidence
ought never to distract us from sadness about this tree, this
landscape, this man's clam bed. Expert talk can easily
deaden our speechless anger over *known* wetlands that have
turned into concrete or asphalt. To speak about the destruction of beauty as an instance of entropy is difficult. The
metaphor tends to hide the sordid wickedness which we
would otherwise deplore, and in which each one who drives
or flies is involved. Words made out of technical terms are
notoriously unfit for metaphorical use. When technical terms
are ferried into an ethical discourse, they almost inevitably
extinguish its moral meaning.

Real *words* have a nimbus. In contrast, *terms* are shorn of
connotations. A nimbus of connotation surrounds words like
a wind chime moved by the voice. Entropy is not such a
word, although many try to use it as one. When it is so used,
it is delimited in two ways: it both loses the sharp edge it had
as a term and it never acquires the overtones of a strong
word. In a poem it is a stone and in a political discourse a
cudgel.

The words people use when they want to say something of
importance are neither arbitrarily picked from a dead language — like ancient Greek — nor given their meaning only
through definition. Each genuine word has its native place; it
is rooted like a plant in a meadow. Some words spread like
creepers, others are like hardwood. But what they do is
under the control of the speaker. Each speaker tries to make
his words mean what he wants to say. But there is no clear
meaning in entropy when it is not used as the name of a
cypher. No one can tell the person who utters this word with
his mouth that he uses it wrongly. There is no right way to
use a technical term in ordinary conversation.

When 'entropy' is used as part of ordinary speech, it loses the power to name a formula: it fits neither sentence nor system. But it also lacks the kind of connotation that strong words have. The term gives off a halo of evocation that, unlike the meanings of sound words, is vague and arbitrary. When 'entropy' appears in a political statement the usage gives the impression of being scientific while in fact it is probably meaningless. If it convinces, it does so not by its own strength but by irrational seduction. It veils a moral perversion from which the speaker would otherwise recoil because it gives the impression that something weighty and scientific is being said.

What I see, what I cry over, what deeply disturbs me on that degraded island of Okinawa is the result of presumption, aggression and human greed. Entropy powerfully suggests a strict analogy between the realm of human dignity and freedom and cosmic laws. By speaking about aggression, greed and despair within the context of entropy, I excuse crime and carelessness by evoking cosmic necessity. Instead of confessing that I advance an evil through my own lifestyle, I suggest that the elimination of beauty and variety is the unavoidable way of, equally, nature and culture. This is the issue about which Tamanoy spoke out. He defined the ideologically shaped local interaction of man and earth as the center of the cosmos.

Yet in spite of this ambiguity, entropy remains a valuable word. When used as a suggestive, ever-limping metaphor, rather than as a reductive analogy, it serves to alert some to social degradation, the loss of beauty and variety, growing triviality and squalor. It helps us to recognize random noise; the senseless and meaningless waves that bombard all our inner and outer senses. If I could be sure that its limitations were kept in mind, I would not want to lose it.

Disvalue versus entropy

When taken literally, metaphors produce absurdities. To insist that my child's brain is a computer expresses nothing more than a trendy paternal vanity. Yet much of a meta-phor's effectiveness comes from the shock evoked in the hearer by an intentional misuse of language. And metaphor works only when the two realms between which this meta-ferry plies are shores within the reach of the hearer. Now, there could hardly be more distant and obscure realms than those which entropy as metaphor seeks to connect. For the typical listener, the world of science is formidable — by definition, its mathematical language is foreign to the man on the street. On the other hand, the realm in which the metaphor of entropy is supposed to act as a guide — the universe of monitored pollution, apocalyptic security, pro-grammed education, medicalized sickness, computer-managed death and other forms of institutionalized non-sense — is so frightening that I can only face it with the respect due the devil; a constant fear of losing my heart's sensitivity by becoming accustomed to evil.

This is the danger associated with using the term 'entropy', for the frustrating and pervasive socio-economic twist that morally perverts almost every aspect of postmod-ern life. And yet the word did us a favor. It forced us to recognize that we are speechless in the face of a social evolution which (falsely) gives the impression of being as natural as the hypothetical chaos resulting from the irrevers-able run of the universe.

The word that names this twist ought to be one that includes the historical and moral nature of our sadness, the perfidy and depravity that cause the loss of beauty, of autonomy and of that dignity which makes human labor worthy. Entropy implies that despoliation is a cosmic law, which started with the Big Bang. The social degradation that must be named is not co-equal with the universe, but something which had a beginning in mankind's history and which, for this reason, might be brought to an end.

I propose 'disvalue' as the appropriate word. Disvalue can be related to the degradation of value as entropy has been related to the degradation of energy. Entropy is a measure of the transformation of energy into a form that can no longer be converted into physical 'work'. 'Disvalue' is a term that bespeaks the wasting of commons and culture with the result that traditional labor is voided of its power to generate subsistence. On this point the analogy between the two concepts is close enough to justify the metaphorical jump from astronomy to modern lifestyles and back.

I know well that the word 'disvalue' is not in the dictionaries. You can devalue something which was formerly held to be precious: stocks can lose their value; old coins can rise in value; critical sociology can take a value-neutral stance; feigned love can be valueless. In all these applications of value the speaker takes 'value' for granted. In current usage, then, value can stand for almost anything. Indeed, it can be used to replace the good. It is born from the same mind set which in the third quarter of the last century also brought forth 'labor force', 'waste', 'energy' and 'entropy'.

By coining the concept of disvalue both the homologies and the contradictions that exist between social and physical degradation can be shown. While physical 'work' tends to increase entropy, the economic productivity of work is based on the previous dis-valuation of cultural labor. Waste and degradation are usually considered as side effects in the production of values. I suggest precisely the opposite. I argue that economic value accumulates only as the result of the previous wasting of culture, which can also be considered as the creation of disvalue.

The parable of Mexico's 'waste'

Mexico City presents the world with a new plague. In this place salmonella and amoebas are now routinely transmitted through the respiratory tract. When you first arrive in the valley of Technochtitlán, surrounded by mountains and 8,000 feet above sea level, you inevitably struggle to breathe the thin air. Half a century ago it was crisp, clean air. What you now draw into your lungs is an atmosphere heavily polluted by a smog containing a high density of solid particles, many of which are pathogenic agents. A specific set of social conditions incubates and disperses the city's bacteria. Some of these illustrate how cultural breakdown, ideology and university-bred prejudice combine to create disvalue. The evolution of Mexico City during the last three decades is a cautionary tale describing the highly productive manufacture of disvalue.

In the last four decades, the city grew from one to over twenty million persons. The single experience which most newcomers share before their arrival is nearly unlimited open space. Pre-Columbian agriculture did not use large domestic animals. Cow, horse and donkey were imports from Europe. Animal droppings were at a premium. The dispersal of human excrements was the rule. Most of the recent immigrants come from rural areas. They do not possess inbred toilet habits appropriate for a densely populated habitat. And Mexican notions of defecation have never been shaped by the attention paid to these matters by Hindu, Muslim or Confucian disciplines. No wonder that in Mexico City today between four and five million people lack any proper place to deposit their stool, urine and blood. The ideology of the W.C. paralyzes the cultural urbanization of patterns native to the immigrants.

Elitist blindness to the cultural nature of excrements, when these are produced in a modern city, is compounded by highly specialized fantasies implanted in the minds of Mexican bureaucrats by international schools of hygiene. The Anglo-Saxon prejudice that physiologically blocks bowel movements unless one sits over water with a roll of paper at hand has become endemic among the Mexican governing élite. As a result, the Mexican leadership is singularly blind to the real issue at hand. Further, this élite was stimulated to megalomanic planning during the oil boom of the early seventies. At that time, huge public works were undertaken which were never completed, and the ruins of unfinished projects are taken as symbols of development which will soon restart. While many of the poor move on, recognizing that the end of development is at hand, the government continues to speak of a temporary economic crisis that has momentarily throttled the flow of dollars and water. Toilet training, combined with the illusion of living in a short-term crisis, blinds the planners and sanitation experts to the evidence that the body excrements of their four million toilet-less neighbors will only continue to remain, rot and atomize in the thin air of the high plateau.

The Mexican earthquake

Then, in September, 1985, an earthquake shook not only the capital but also the complacency of some professionals. Engineers and health planners in countries like Mexico almost inevitably belong to the class who, by definition, use the W.C. But in 1985 many of these had no water at home or at work for several weeks. For the first time, some editorial writers began to question whether hygiene inevitably means the dilution of feces and the generation of black water. What should have been obvious long ago suddenly became evident conclusions for a few: it is beyond the economic power of Mexico to provide water for several million additional toilets. Further, even if there were enough money and stringent rules applied on the use of flush, the generalization of the W.C. would be a serious and disastrous aggression against rural Mexico. The attempt to pump the necessary millions of gallons would devastate the semi-arid farm communities within a radius of more than a hundred miles. It would thus force new millions into the city. Then thousands of acres of fragile soil on the terraces, some built before the Spaniards, if left untended, would wash away. The center of the Meso-American plateau would become a permanent desert. All this loss would be the result of an ideology that treats humans as natural waste producers. Thinking differently, a new political opposition arose and picked up the slogan of composting units for rich and poor.

It was interesting to observe how this small but potentially influential group reacted in the absence of the toilet ideology. The ideal of *la normalidad*, which in Spanish means perpendicularity, went to pieces for them. These people, including some professionals but most quite poor, prisoners of the world's greatest megacity, rejected the symbols of urban life, such as skyscrapers, deep tunnels and monster markets. The ruins of the inner city became for them a sign of hope. Hitherto unexamined certainties about water and excrement became the source of laughter. Economic development became the butt of jokes in the *pulquerias*. Obviously it did not lead to the distribution of accumulated value, but to the generation of a huge turd composed of cement and plastic needing to be tended by professional services. Sewers became the symbol for remedies required in a city set up for the economic toilet training of *homo œconomicus*.

The history of waste

The social definition of excrements, which in the opinion of those who generate them cannot be turned into compost, has become a cypher for the junking of people. The latter learn that they depend on services even when they act under the urge of the most elementary needs. In this perspective, the W.C. is a device to instill the habit of self-junking or self-disvaluation, which prepares one for dependence on scarce services in other spheres. It brings into existence the body percept of *homo* the generator of waste. When people grasp that several times a day their physical needs for evacuation produce a degradation of the environment, it is easy to convince them that by their very existence they cannot but contribute to 'entropy'.

Waste is not the natural consequence of human existence. Professor Ludolf Kuchenbuch, who is working on a history of waste, has gathered the evidence. A concept that we take for granted does not appear before 1830. Before that date 'waste', as a verb and as a noun, is related to devastation, destruction, desertification, degradation. It is not something that can be removed. Professors Tamanoy and Murata have built their theory on a similar assumption: if a culture steadily enhances the interaction of sun, soil and water, its net contribution to the cosmos is positive. Human societies that create waste are those which destroy the soil-water matrix of their locality and become expansive centers for the devastation of those around them. Entropy appears as a result of the destruction of cultures and their commons.

It is therefore unwarranted to attribute waste management to all cultures. Miasma and taboo are in no way ancestors of modern pollution. They are the symbolic rules that enhance integration and protect subsistence cultures. So-called development is a programmed disvaluation of these protections.

Disvalue versus waste

Disvalue remains invisible as long as two conditions obtain. The first of these consists in the widespread belief that economic categories, whose task it is to measure 'values', can be used in statements about communities whose 'business' is not values but *the good*. The good is part of a local 'ideology' related to the mixture of elements native to a specific place — to speak with Paracelsus or Tamanoy — while values are a measure which fits the abstract ideology of science. The second source of blindness to disvalue is an obsessive certainty about the feasibility of progress. This reduction of conviviality to primitive economics and the abhorrence of tradition, masked as a commitment to the progress of others, together foster the myopic destruction of the past. Tradition comes to be seen as a historical expression of waste, to be discarded with the trash of the past.

Only a decade ago it still seemed possible to speak of twentieth-century progress with assurance. The economy appeared to be a machine that increases the flow of money. Energy, information and money all seemed to follow the same rules — the laws of entropy were equally applicable to each. The development of productive capacity, multiplication of trained workers and rise in savings were seen as parts of 'growth' which, sooner or later, would bring more money to more people. In spite of wider social disintegration due to the increase of money flow, ever more money was proposed as the fundamental requirement to satisfy the basic needs of more people! Entropy then seemed a tempting analog for the social degradation resulting from the pervasive flow.

In the meantime, a new and radical questioning of economic verities began. As recently as twenty years ago, it was not yet ridiculous to look for a world community based on equal dignity and fairness that could be planned on the thermodynamic model of value flows. This is no longer so in the mid-eighties. Not only the promise of human equality, but even the provision of an equal chance for survival, sounds hollow. On a world scale it is obvious that growth has concentrated economic benefits, simultaneously disvaluing people and places, in such a way that survival has become impossible outside the money economy. More people are more destitute and helpless than ever before. Further, those privileges which only higher income can buy are increasingly valued primarily as an escape from the disvalue which affects the lives of all.

The ideology of economic progress throws a shadow of disvalue on almost all activities that are culturally shaped outside of money flow. People like the immigrants to Mexico City, and beliefs such as those in local health rules, are de-valued long before effective toilets can be provided. People are forced into a new mental topology in which locations for bowel movements are scarce, even though resources to create these places are beyond the reasonable reach of the new economy in which they find themselves. The ideology of production and consumption under the implied condition of 'natural' scarcity takes hold of their minds while neither paid jobs nor money are attainable for them. Self-degradation, self-junking, self-wasting are different ways to name this creation of the necessary conditions for the legitimate growth of a money economy.

This is where Joshiro Tamanoy comes in. He not only translated but he taught Karl Polanyi. He picked up the distinction between formal and substantive economies that goes back to Polanyi. Forty years after Polanyi, Tamanoy — whom I know only from conversation, since most of his writings are in a language of which I am ignorant — brought this distinction into modern Japan. It can be used to sum up our argument. Entropy is probably an effective metaphor to stress de-valuation in the formal economy. The flow of money or information can in some way be compared to the flow of heat. But it is now obvious that macro-economics tells us nothing about what people consider *good*. Therefore, entropy cannot be relevant to explain the devastation of substantive cultural patterns by which people act outside the formal money economy. This is true because the 'exchange' of gifts or movements of goods in the substantive economy are, by their very nature, heterogeneous to the flow-model of values postulated by a formal economy. And, as the thermo-dynamic flow model spreads, it extinguishes a way of life to which entropy will forever be foreign.

The Three Dimensions of Public Option

Keynote Speech at the 16th General Assembly
of the Society for International Development
Colombo, Sri Lanka, 15th August 1979

Where sixteen years of your war against subsistence have led can best be seen in the mirror of development. During the sixties, 'development' acquired a status that ranked with 'freedom' and 'equality.' Other people's development became the rich man's duty and burden. Development was described as a building program — people of all colors spoke of 'nation-building' and did so without blushing. The immediate goal of this social engineering was the installation of a balanced set of equipment in a society not yet so instrumented: the building of more schools, more hospitals, more highways, new factories, power grids, together with the creation of a population trained to staff and need them.

The Nemesis of development

Today, the moral imperative of ten years ago appears naive; today, few critical thinkers would take such an instrumentalist view of the desirable society. A host of reasons have changed people's minds: *undesired externalities* exceed benefits — the tax burden of schools and hospitals is more than most economies can support; the ghost towns produced by highways impoverish the urban and rural landscape; although plastic buckets from São Paulo are lighter and cheaper than those made of scrap by the local tin-smith in Western Brazil, they put the tin-smith out of existence, and the fumes of the plastic leave a special trace on the environment — a new kind of ghost. The destruction of age-old competence as well as these poisons are *inevitable byproducts* and will resist all exorcisms for a long time. Cemeteries for industrial wastes simply cost too much, more than the buckets are worth. In economic jargon, the 'external costs' exceed not only the profit made from plastic bucket production, but also the very salaries paid in the manufacturing process.

These rising externalities, however, are only one side of the bill which development has exacted. *Counterproductivity is its reverse side.* Externalities represent costs that are 'outside' the price paid by the consumer for what he wants — costs that he, others or future generations will at some point be charged. Counterproductivity, however, is a new kind of disappointment which arises 'within' the very use of the good purchased. This internal counterproductivity, an inevitable component of modern institutions, has become the constant frustration of the poorer majority of each institution's clients: intensely experienced but rarely defined. Each major sector of the economy produces its own unique and paradoxical contradictions. Each necessarily effects the opposite of that for which it was structured. Economists, who are increasingly competent to put price-tags on externalities, are unable to deal with negative internalities and cannot measure the inherent frustration of captive clients which is something other than a cost. For most people, schooling twists genetic differences into certified degradation; the medicalization of health increases demand for services far beyond the possible and useful, and undermines that organic coping ability which common sense calls health; transportation, for the great majority bound to the rush hour, increases the time spent in the servitude to traffic, reducing both freely chosen mobility and mutual access. The development of educational, medical and other welfare agencies has actually removed most clients from the obvious purpose for which these projects were designed and financed. This institutionalized frustration, resulting from compulsory consumption, combines with the new externalities. It demands an increase in the production of scavenging and repair services to impoverish and even destroy individuals and communities, affecting them in a class-specific manner. The peculiarly modern forms of frustration and paralysis and destruction totally discredit the description of the desirable society in terms of installed production capacity.

Defense against the damages inflicted by development, rather than access to some new 'satisfaction,' has become the most sought-after privilege. You have arrived if you can commute outside the rush hour; probably attended an élite school, if you can give birth at home; are privy to rare and special knowledge if you can bypass the physician when you are ill; are rich and lucky if you can breathe fresh air; by no means poor, if you can build your own shack. The underclasses are now made up of those who *must* consume the counterproductive packages and ministrations of their self-appointed tutors; the privileged are those who are free to refuse them. A new attitude, then, has taken shape during these last years. The awareness that we cannot ecologically afford *equitable* development leads many to understand that, even if development in equity were possible, we would neither want more of it for ourselves, nor want to suggest it for others.

Dimensions of redress

Ten years ago, we tended to distinguish social options exercised within the political sphere from technical options assigned to the expert. The former were meant to focus on goals, the latter more on means. Roughly, options about the desirable society were ranged on a spectrum that ran from right to left: here capitalist, over there, socialist 'development.' The *how* was left to the experts. This one-dimensional model of politics is now passé. Today, in addition to 'who gets what,' two new areas of choice have become *lay* issues: the very legitimacy of lay judgment on the apt means for production, and the trade-offs between growth and freedom. As a result, three independent classes of options appear as three mutually perpendicular axes of public choice. On the x-axis I place the issues related to social hierarchy, political authority, ownership of the means of production and allocation of resources that are usually designated by the terms, right and left. On the y-axis, I place the technical choices between hard and soft, extending these terms far beyond pro and con atomic power: not only goods, but also services are affected by the hard and soft alternatives.

A third choice falls on the z-axis. Neither privilege nor technique, but rather the nature of human satisfaction, is at issue. To characterize the two extremes, I shall use terms defined by Erich Fromm. At the bottom, I place a social organization that fits the seeking of satisfaction in *having*; at the top, in *doing*. At the bottom, therefore, I place a commodity-intensive society where needs are increasingly defined in terms of packaged goods and services designed and prescribed by professionals and produced under their control. This social ideal corresponds to the image of a humanity composed of individuals, each driven by considerations of marginal utility, the image that has developed from Mandeville via Smith and Marx to Keynes, and that Louis Dumont calls *homo œconomicus*. At the opposite end, at the top of the z-axis, I place — in a fan-shaped array — a great variety of subsistence activities. In its unique way, each of these cannot but be skeptical about the claims of growth. In such new societies where contemporary tools ease the creation of use-values, commodities and industrial production in general are deemed valuable mainly insofar as they are either resources or instruments for subsistence. Hence, the social ideal corresponds to *homo habilis*, an image which includes numerous individuals who are *differently* competent at coping with reality, the opposite of *homo œconomicus*, who is dependent on standardized 'needs.' Here, people who choose their independence and their own horizon derive more satisfaction from doing and making things for immediate use than from the products of slaves or machines. Therefore, every cultural project is necessarily modest. Here, people go as far as they can toward self-subsistence, producing themselves what they can, exchanging their surplus with neighbors, avoiding —insofar as possible — the products of wage-labor.

The shape of contemporary society is the result of the ongoing choices along these three independent axes. And a polity's credibility today depends on the degree of public participation in each of the three option sets. The beauty of a unique, socially articulated image of each society will, hopefully, become the determining factor of its international impact. Esthetic and ethical example may replace the competition of economic indicators. Actually, no other route is open. A mode of life characterized by austerity, modesty, constructed by hard work and built on a small scale does not lend itself to propagation through marketing. For the first time in history, poor and rich societies would be effectively placed on equal terms. But for this to become true, the present perception of international North-South relations in terms of development must first be superseded.

The Rise and fall of wage-labor

A related high status goal of our age, full employment, must also be reviewed. Ten years ago, attitudes toward development and politics were simpler than is possible today; attitudes toward work were sexist and naive. Work was identified with employment, and prestigious employment confined to males. The analysis of shadow work done off the job was taboo. The left referred to it as a remnant of primitive reproduction, the right, as organized consumption. All agreed that, with development, such labor would wither away. The struggle for more jobs, for equal pay for equal jobs, and more pay for every job pushed all work done off the job into a shadowed corner hidden from politics and economics. Recently, feminists, together with some economists and sociologists, looking at so-called intermediary structures, have begun to examine the unpaid contribution made to an industrial economy, a contribution for which women are principally responsible. These persons discuss 'reproduction' as the complement to production. But the stage is mostly filled with self-styled radicals who discuss new ways of creating conventional jobs, new forms of sharing available jobs and how to transform housework, education, childbearing and commuting into paid jobs. Under the pressure of such demands, the full employment goal appears as dubious as development.

New actors, who question the very nature of work, advance toward the limelight. They distinguish industrially structured work, paid or unpaid, from the creation of a livelihood beyond the confines of employment and professional tutors. Their discussions raise the key issues on the vertical axis. The choice for or against the notion of man as a growth addict decides whether unemployment, that is, the effective liberty to work free from wages or salary, shall be viewed as sad and a curse, or as useful and a right.

In a commodity-intensive society, basic needs are met through the products of wage-labor — housing no less than education, traffic no less than the delivery of infants. The work ethic which drives such a society legitimates employment for salary or wages and degrades independent coping. But the spread of wage-labor accomplishes more — it divides unpaid work into two opposite types of activities. While the loss of unpaid work through the encroachment of wage-labor has often been described, the creation of a new kind of work has been consistently ignored: the unpaid *complement* of industrial labor and services. A kind of forced labor or industrial serfdom in the service of commodity-intensive economies must be carefully distinguished from subsistence-oriented work lying outside the industrial system. Unless this distinction is clarified and used when choosing options on the z-axis, unpaid work guided by professionals could spread through a repressive, ecological welfare society. Women's serfdom in the domestic sphere is the most obvious example today. Housework is not salaried. Nor is it a subsistence activity in the sense that most of the work done by women was such as when, with their menfolk, they used the entire household as the setting and the means for the creation of most of the inhabitants' livelihood. Modern housework is standardized by industrial commodities oriented toward the support of production, and exacted from women in a sex-specific way to press them into reproduction, regeneration and a motivating force for the wage-laborer. Well publicized by feminists, housework is only one expression of that extensive shadow economy which has developed everywhere in industrial societies as a necessary complement to expanding wage-labor. This shadow complement, together with the formal economy, is a constitutive element of the industrial mode of production. It has escaped economic analysis, as did the wave nature of elementary particles before the Quantum Theory. And when concepts developed for the formal economic sector are applied to it, they distort what they do not simply miss. The real difference between two kinds of unpaid activity — shadow work which complements wage-labor, and subsistence work which competes with and opposes both — is consistently missed. Then, as subsistence activities become more rare, all unpaid activities assume a structure analogous to housework. Growth-oriented work inevitably leads to the standardization and management of activities, be they paid or unpaid.

A contrary view of work prevails when a community chooses a subsistence-oriented way of life. There, the inversion of development, the replacement of consumer goods by personal action, of industrial tools by convivial tools is the goal. There, both wage-labor and shadow work will decline since their product, goods or services, is valued primarily as a means for ever-inventive activities, rather than as an end, that is, dutiful consumption. There, the guitar is valued over the record, the library over the schoolroom, the back yard garden over the supermarket. There, the personal control of each worker over his means of production determines the small horizon of each enterprise, a horizon which is a necessary condition for social production and the unfolding of each worker's individuality. This mode of production also exists in slavery, serfdom and other forms of dependence. But it flourishes, releases its energy, acquires its adequate and classical form *only* where the worker is the free owner of his tools and resources; only then can the artisan perform like a virtuoso. This mode of production can be maintained only within the limits that nature dictates to both production and society. There, useful unemployment is valued while wage-labor, within limits, is merely tolerated.

Commodity dependence

The development paradigm is more easily repudiated by those who were adults on January 10, 1949. That day, most of us met the term in its present meaning for the first time when President Truman announced his Point Four Program. Until then, we used 'development' to refer to species, real estate and moves in chess — only thereafter to people, countries and economic strategies. Since then, we have been flooded by development theories whose concepts are now curiosities for collectors — 'growth,' 'catching up,' 'modern-ization,' 'imperialism,' 'dualism,' 'dependency,' 'basic needs,' 'transfer of technology,' 'world system,' 'autochtho-nous industrialization' and 'temporary unlinking.' Each onrush came in two waves. One carried the pragmatist who highlighted free enterprise and world markets; the other, the politicians who stressed ideology and revolution. Theorists produced mountains of prescriptions and mutual carica-tures. Beneath these, the common assumptions of all were buried. Now is the time to dig out the axioms hidden in the idea of development itself.

Fundamentally, the concept implies the replacement of general competence and satisfying subsistence activities by the use and consumption of commodities; the monopoly of wage-labor over all other kinds of work; redefinition of needs in terms of goods and services mass-produced according to expert design; finally, the rearrangement of the environment in such fashion that space, time, materials and design favor production and consumption while they degrade or paralyze use-value oriented activities that satisfy needs directly. And all such worldwide homogeneous changes and processes are valued as inevitable and good. The great Mexican muralists dramatically portrayed the typical figures before the theo-rists outlined the stages. On their walls, one sees the ideal type of human being as the male in overalls behind a machine or in a white coat over a microscope. He tunnels mountains, guides tractors, fuels smoking chimneys. Women give him birth, nurse and teach him. In striking contrast to Aztec subsistence, Rivera and Orozco visualize industrial work as the sole source of all the goods needed for life and its possible pleasures.

But this ideal of industrial man now dims. The taboos that protected it weaken. Slogans about the dignity and joy of wage-labor sound tinny. Unemployment, a term first introduced in 1898 to designate people without a fixed income, is now recognized as the condition in which most of the world's people live anyway — even at the height of industrial booms. In Eastern Europe especially, but also in China, people now see that, since 1950, the term, 'working class,' has been used mainly as a cover to claim and obtain privileges for a new bourgeoisie and its children. The 'need' to create employment and stimulate growth, by which the self-appointed paladins of the poorest have so far squashed any consideration of alternatives to development, clearly appears suspect.

Bonded to 'needs'

The challenges to development take multiple forms. In Germany alone, France or Italy, thousands of groups experiment, each differently, with alternatives to an industrial existence. Increasingly, more of these people come from blue-collar homes. For most of them, there is no dignity left in earning one's livelihood by a wage.

They try to 'unplug themselves from consumption,' in the phrase of some South Chicago slum-dwellers. In the United States, at least four million people live in the core of tiny and highly differentiated communities of this kind, with at least seven times as many individually sharing their values — women seek alternatives to gynaecology; parents alternatives to schools; home-builders alternatives to the flush toilet; neighborhoods alternatives to commuting; people alternatives to the shopping center. In Trivandrum, South India, I have seen one of the most successful alternatives to a special kind of commodity dependence — to instruction and certification as the privileged forms of learning. One thousand seven hundred villages have installed libraries, each containing at least a thousand titles. This is the minimum equipment they need to be full members of Kerala Shastra Sahitya Parishad, and they may retain their membership only as long as they loan at least three thousand volumes per year. I was immensely encouraged to see that, at least in South India, village-based and village-financed libraries have turned schools into adjuncts to libraries, while elsewhere libraries have latterly become mere deposits for teaching materials used under the instruction of professional teachers. Also in Bihar, India, Medico International represents a grassroots-based attempt to de-medicalize health care, without falling into the trap of the Chinese barefooted doctor. The latter has been relegated to the lowest-level lackey in a national hierarchy of bio-control.

Besides taking such experimental forms, the challenge to development also uses legal and political means. In an Austrian referendum last year, an absolute majority refused permission to Chancellor Kreisky, politically in control of the electorate, to inaugurate a finished atomic generator. Citizens increasingly use the ballot and the courts, in addition to more traditional interest group pressures, to set negative design criteria for the technology of production. In Europe, 'green' candidates begin to win elections. In America, citizens' legal efforts begin to stop highways and dams. Such behavior was not predictable ten years ago — and many men in power still do not recognize it as legitimate. All these grassroots-organized lives and actions in the metropolis challenge not only the recent concept of overseas development, but also the more fundamental and root concept of progress at home.

Missionaries et al

At this juncture, it is the task of the historian and the

philosopher to clarify the sources of, and disentangle the process resulting in, Western needs. Only thus shall we be able to understand how such a seemingly enlightened concept produced such devastating exploitation. Progress, the notion which has characterized the West for 2000 years and has determined its relations to outsiders since the decay of classical Rome, lies behind the belief in needs. Societies mirror themselves not only in their transcendent gods, but also in their image of the alien beyond their frontiers. The West exported a dichotomy between 'us' and 'them' unique to industrial society. This peculiar attitude towards self and others is now worldwide, constituting the victory of a universalist mission initiated in Europe. A redefinition of development would only reinforce the Western economic domination over the shape of formal economics by the professional colonization of the informal sector, domestic and foreign. To eschew this danger, the six-stage metamorphosis of a concept that currently appears as 'development' must first be understood.

Every community has a characteristic attitude toward others. The Chinese, for example, cannot refer to the alien and his chattel without labeling them with a degrading marker. For the Greek, he is either the house guest from a neighboring polis, or the barbarian who is less than fully a man. In Rome, barbarians could become members of the city, but to bring them into it was never the intent or mission of Rome. Only during late antiquity, with the Western European Church, did the alien become someone in need, someone to be brought in. This view of the alien as a burden has become constitutive for Western society; without this universal mission to the world outside, what we call the West would not have come to be.

The perception of the outsider as someone who must be helped has taken on successive forms. In late antiquity, the barbarian mutated into the pagan — the second stage toward development had begun. The pagan was defined as the unbaptized, but ordained by nature to become Christian. It was the duty of those within the Church to incorporate him by baptism into the body of Christendom. In the early

Middle Ages, most people in Europe were baptized, even though they might not yet be converted. Then the Muslim appeared. Unlike Goths and Saxons, Muslims were monotheists, and obviously prayerful believers; they resisted conversion. Therefore, besides baptism, the further needs to be subjected and instructed had to be imputed. The pagan mutated into the infidel, our third stage. By the late Middle Ages, the image of the alien mutated again. The Moors had been driven from Granada, Columbus had sailed across the ocean, and the Spanish Crown had assumed many functions of the Church. The image of the wild man who threatens the civilizing function of the humanist replaced the image of the infidel who threatens the faith. At this time also, the alien was first described in economy-related terms. From many studies on monsters, apes and wild men, we learn that the Europeans of this period saw the wild man as having no needs. This independence made him noble, but a threat to the designs of colonialism and mercantilism. To impute needs to the wild man, one had to make him over into the native, the fifth stage. Spanish courts, after long deliberation, decided that at least the wild man of the New World had a soul and was, therefore, human. In opposition to the wild man, the native has needs, but needs unlike those of civilized man. His needs are fixed by climate, race, religion and providence. Adam Smith still reflects on the elasticity of native needs. As Gunnar Myrdal has observed, the construct of distinctly native needs was necessary both to justify colonialism and to administer colonies. The provision of government, education and commerce for the natives was for four hundred years the white man's assumed burden.

Each time the West put a new mask on the alien, the old one was discarded because it was now recognized as a caricature of an abandoned self-image. The pagan with his naturally Christian soul had to give way to the stubborn infidel to allow Christendom to launch the Crusades. The wild man became necessary to justify the need for secular humanist education. The native was the crucial concept to promote self-righteous colonial rule. But by the time of the Marshall Plan, when multinational conglomerates were expanding and the ambitions of transnational pedagogues, therapists and planners knew no bounds, the natives' limited need for goods and services thwarted growth and progress. They had to metamorphose into underdeveloped people, the sixth and present stage of the West's view of the outsider. Thus decolonization was also a process of conversion: the worldwide acceptance of the Western self-image of *homo œconomicus* in his most extreme form as *homo industrialis*, with all needs commodity-defined. Scarcely twenty years were enough to make two billion people define themselves as underdeveloped. I vividly remember the Rio Carnival of 1963 — the last before the Junta imposed itself. 'Development' was the motif in the prize-winning samba, 'development' the shout of the dancers while they jumped to the throbbing of the drums.

Development based on high per capita energy quanta and intense professional care is the most pernicious of the West's missionary efforts — a project guided by an ecologically unfeasible conception of human control over nature, and by an anthropologically vicious attempt to replace the nests and snakepits of culture by sterile wards for professional service. The hospitals that spew out the newborn and re-absorb the dying, the schools run to busy the unemployed before, between and after jobs, the apartment towers where people are stored between trips to the supermarkets, the highways connecting garages form a pattern tattooed into the landscape during the short development spree. These institutions, designed for lifelong bottle babies wheeled from medical center to school to office to stadium begin now to look as anomalous as cathedrals, albeit unredeemed by any esthetic charm.

Ecological and anthropological realism are now necessary — but with caution. The popular call for soft is ambiguous; both right and left appropriate it. On the z-axis, it equally serves a honeyed beehive, or the pluralism of independent actions. The soft choice easily permits a recasting of a maternal society at home and another metamorphosis of missionary zeal abroad. For example, Amory Lovins argues that the possibility of further growth now depends on a rapid transition to the soft path. Only in this way, he claims, can the real income of rich countries double and that of poor countries triple in this generation. Only by the transition from fossil to sun can the externalities of production be so cut that the resources now spent on making waste and hiring scavengers to remove it be turned into benefits. I agree. If growth is to be, then Lovins is right; and investments are more secure with windspinners than with oil derricks.

Shadow work

The World Bank makes the matching argument for services. Only by choosing labor-intensive, sometimes less efficient forms of industrial production can education be incorporated in apprenticeship. More efficient plants create huge and costly externalities in the formal education they presuppose, while they cannot teach on the job.

The World Health Organization now stresses prevention and education for self-care. Only in this way can population health levels be raised, while expensive therapies — mostly of unproven effectiveness, although still the principal work of physicians — can be abandoned. The liberal egalitarian utopia of the eighteenth century, taken up as the ideal for industrial society by the socialists of the nineteenth, now seems realizable only on the soft and self-help path. On this point, right and left converge. Wolfgang Harich, a highly cultured Communist, refined and steeled in his conviction by two stretches of eight years in solitary confinement — once under Hitler and once under Ulbricht — is the one East European spokesman for the soft path. But while for Lovins the transition to decentralized production depends on the market, for Harich the necessity of this transition is an argument in favor of Stalinist ecology. For right *and* left, democrats *or* authoritarians, soft process and energy become the necessary means to satisfy escalating 'needs' through the standardized production of goods and services.

Thus, the soft path can lead either toward a convivial society where people are so equipped to do on their own whatever they judge necessary for survival and pleasure, or toward a new kind of commodity-dependent society where the goal of full employment means the political management of activities, paid or unpaid. Whether a 'left' or 'soft' path leads toward or away from new forms of 'development' and 'full employment' depends on the options taken between 'having' and 'being' on the third axis.

We have seen that wherever wage-labor expands, its shadow, industrial serfdom, also grows. Wage-labor, as the dominant form of production, and housework, as the ideal type of its unpaid complement, are both forms of activity without precedent in history or anthropology. They thrive only where the absolute and, later, the industrial state destroyed the social conditions for subsistence living. They spread as small-scale, diversified, vernacular communities were made sociologically and legally impossible — into a world where individuals, throughout their lives, live only through dependence on education, health services, transportation and other packages provided through the multiple mechanical feeders of industrial institutions.

Conventional economic analysis has focused on only one of these complementary industrial age activities. Economic analysis has focused on the worker as wage-earning producer. The equally commodity-oriented activities performed by the unemployed have remained in the shadow of the economic searchlight. What women or children do, what occupies men after 'working hours,' is belittled in a cavalier fashion. But this is changing rapidly. Both the weight and the nature of the contribution made by unpaid activities to the industrial system begin to be noticed. Feminist research into the history and anthropology of work has made it impossible to ignore the fact that work in an industrial society is sex-specific in a manner which cuts deeper than in any other known society. In the nineteenth century, women entered the wage-labor force in the 'advanced' nations; they then won the franchise, non-restricted access to schooling, and equal rights on the job. All these 'victories' have had precisely the opposite effect from that which conventional wisdom assigns them. Paradoxically, 'emancipation' has heightened the contrast between paid and unpaid work; it has severed all connections between unpaid work and subsistence. Thus, it has redefined the structure of unpaid work so that this latter becomes a new kind of serfdom inevitably borne by women.

Gender-specific tasks are not new; all known societies assign sex-specific work roles. For example, hay may be cut by men, raked by women, gathered by men, loaded by women, carted away by men, fed to cows by women and to horses by men. But no matter how much we search other cultures, we cannot find the contemporary division between two forms of work, one paid and the other unpaid, one credited as productive and the other as concerned with reproduction and consumption, one considered heavy and the other light, one demanding special qualifications and the other not, one given high social prestige and the other relegated to 'private' matters. Both are equally fundamental in the industrial mode of production. They differ in that the surplus from paid work is taxed directly by the employer, while the added value of unpaid work reaches him only via wage-work. Nowhere can we find two such distinct forms through which, in each family, surplus is created and expropriated.

Colonization of the 'informal sector'

This division between unpaid work off the job and paid work through employment would have been unthinkable in societies where the whole house served as a framework in which its inhabitants, to a large extent, did and made those things by which they also lived. Although we can find traces of both wage-work and its shadow in many societies, in none could either become the society's paradigm of work, nor be used as the key symbol for sex-specific tasks. And since two such types of work did not exist, the family did not have to exist to couple these kinds of opposites. Nowhere in history is the family, nuclear or extended, the instrument for linking two complementary but mutually exclusive species of work, one assigned primarily to the male, the other to the female. This symbiosis between opposite forms of activity, inseparably wedded through the family, is unique to commodity-intensive society. We now see that it is the inevitable result of the pursuit of development and full employment. And since such kinds of work did not exist, sex-roles could not be defined with such finality, distinct natures could not be attributed to male and female, families could not be transformed into a solder to weld the two together.

A feminist analysis of the history of industrial work thus removes the blindspot of economics: *homo œconomicus* has never been sexually neutral; *homo industrialis* appeared from the beginning in two genders: *vir laborans*, the workingman, and *femina domestica*, the *Hausfrau*. In no society that developed toward the goal of full employment has shadow work not grown apace with employment. And shadow work provided a device, effective beyond every precedent, to degrade a type of activity in which women cannot but predominate, while it supported one which privileged men.

Quite recently, the orthodox distinction between production and consumption functions ceased to hold. Suddenly, opposing interests turn the importance of unpaid work into a public issue. Economists put shadow prices on what happens in the 'informal' sector; the contribution that the work done by the client in choosing, paying for and carrying his cake adds to the value of the cake; the calculus of marginal choices made in sexual activities; the value of jogging over heart surgery.

Housewives claim pay for housework at the rate for such services in motels and restaurants. Teachers transmogrify mothers into trained but unpaid supervisors of their own children's homework. Government reports recognize that basic needs as professionally defined can be met only if laymen also produce these services, with competence but without pay. If growth and full employment retain their status as goals, the management of disciplined people motivated by non-monetary rewards will open up as the latest form of 'development' in the 1980's.

Down to earth

Rather than life in a shadow economy, I propose, on top of the z-axis, the idea of vernacular work: unpaid activities which provide and improve livelihood, but which are totally refractory to any analysis utilizing concepts developed in formal economics. I apply the term 'vernacular' to these activities, since there is no other current concept that allows me to make the same distinction within the domain covered by such terms as 'informal sector,' 'use value,' 'social reproduction.' Vernacular is a Latin term that we use in English only for the language that we have acquired without paid teachers. In Rome, it was used from 500 B.C. to 600 A.D. to designate any value that was homebred, homemade, derived from the commons, and that a person could protect and defend though he neither bought nor sold it in the market. I suggest that we restore this simple term, vernacular, to oppose commodities and their shadow. It allows me to distinguish between the expansion of the shadow economy and its inverse — the expansion of the vernacular domain.

The tension and balance between vernacular work and industrial labor — paid and unpaid — is the key issue on the third dimension of options, distinct from political right and left and from technical soft and hard. Industrial labor, paid and otherwise exacted, will not disappear. But when development, wage-labor and its shadow encroach upon vernacular work, the relative priority of one or the other constitutes the issue. We are free to choose between hierarchically managed standardized work that may be paid or unpaid, self-selected or imposed on the one hand and, on the other, we can protect our freedom to choose ever newly invented forms of simple, integrated subsistence actions which have an outcome that is unpredictable to the bureaucrat, unmanageable by hierarchies and oriented to the values shared within a specific community.

If the economy expands, which the soft choice can permit, the shadow economy cannot but grow even faster, and the vernacular domain must further decline. In this case, with rising job scarcity, the unemployed will be integrated into newly organized useful activities in the informal sector. Unemployed men will be given the so-called privilege to engage in those production-fostering types of unpaid activity that, since their emergence as housework in the nineteenth century, have been considerably earmarked for the 'weaker sex' — a designation that was also first used at that time, when industrial serfdom rather than subsistence was defined as the task of women. 'Care' exacted for the sake of love will lose its sex-specific character, and in the process will become manageable by the state.

Under *this* option, international development is here to stay. Technical aid to develop the informal sector overseas will reflect the new sexless unpaid domestication of the unemployed at home. The new experts pushing French rather than German self-help methods or windmill designs already crowd airports and conference halls. The last hope of development bureaucracies lies in the development of shadow economies.

Many of the dissidents that I have mentioned take a stand against all this — against the use of soft technology to reduce the vernacular domain and to increase professional controls over informal sector activities. These new vanguards conceive technical progress as one possible instrument to support a new type of value, neither traditional nor industrial, but both subsistence-oriented and rationally chosen. Their lives, with more and less success, express a critical sense of beauty, a particular experience of pleasure, a unique view of life cherished by one group, understood but not necessarily shared by the next. They have found that modern tools make it possible to subsist on activities which permit a variety of evolving lifestyles and relieve much of the drudgery of old time subsistence. They struggle for the freedom to expand the vernacular domain of their lives.

Examples from Travancore to Wales may soon free those majorities who were recently captivated by the modern 'demonstration model' of stupefying, sickening and paralyzing enrichment. But two conditions must be met. First the mode of life resulting from a new relation between people and tools must be informed by the perception of man as *homo*

UNIVERSITY COLLEGE
LIBRARY
SWANSEA

habilis and not *homo industrialis*. Second, commodity-independent lifestyles must be shaped anew by each small community, and not be imposed. Communities living by predominantly vernacular values have nothing much to offer to others besides the attractiveness of their examples. But the example of a poor society that enhances modern subsistence by vernacular work should be rather attractive to jobless males in a rich society now condemned, like their women, to social reproduction in an expanding shadow economy. The ability, however, not only to live in new ways, but to insist on this freedom, demands that we clearly recognize what distinguishes the perception of *homo œconomicus* from all other human beings. To this end I choose the study of history as a privileged road.

PART TWO

The Educational Sphere

Fragment from notes for a lecture at Teachers College, Columbia University, New York. Spring 1979

I distinguish taught mother tongue and the process by which it is learned from vernacular language and the development of competence in its use. The former results from both formal and informal educational activities, while the concepts of pedagogics developed since the sixteenth century are only metaphorically applicable to the latter, the vernacular domain. By describing in general terms the limited appropriateness of pedagogical concepts to learning in primitive cultures, learning in pre-industrial societies and, particularly, learning of certain competences in modern, commodity-intensive economies, I use insights gained through contemporary economic history and anthropology and apply them to the field of education. The inapplicability of pedagogical concepts to the learning of vernacular language can then be extended to other areas of learning, and the implicit limits to all education can then be understood. I hope to encourage research *on* as distinct from research *in* education, that is, research that examines the myths, the practices, the structures and the assumptions that are now common to all societies where education has been 'disembedded' as a distinct realm of activity, as a formal context or sphere.

The medieval mind firmly accepted the existence of heavenly spheres; the contemporary mind as certainly adheres to the existence of social spheres. My argument focuses especially on the educational spheres, but it can be generalized to the other modern spheres. On each of these spheres, two types of research can be done: that which does not go beyond the model of Copernicus, and that which tends to resemble the work of Kepler. The former is concerned with exploring the possible restructuring of the educational (or other) sphere by redefining its centerpiece, recalculating its amplitude, integrating more epicycles into its curriculum, or reassigning to it a new place or order within the hierarchy of social spheres. The latter research searches for the origins of the paradigm itself and, therefore, implicitly recognizes that, like heavenly spheres, modern social spheres might one day disappear.

Astronomers deal with a before and an after. They know that at some date human beings were able to reckon with a Copernican and then with a relativistic sky. They remember the change when planets were first perceived as physical objects that spin around the sun. They work within a paradigm that has an acknowledged beginning and, therefore, can plausibly end. Educators still lack such a historical perspective on their own work. The sphere of their competence appears to them as beginningless. They now need to recall that Ptolemy no less than Copernicus, Aristotle no less than Thomas Aquinas, were all convinced that planets were embedded in crystal spheres — transparent, hollow, perfect globes moving in uniform fashion. According to Aquinas, science was free to investigate, first, if heavenly spheres were driven by a soul, second, precisely how many spheres there were, and third, to what degree these spheres and their epicycles were eccentric. However, their existence, their substantive, three-dimensional nature, and their uniform circular motion could not be questioned without upsetting sound philosophical truth — and the latter was needed for the explanation of Christian dogma. Today, these men's common, firm and critical conviction about the existence of such heavenly spheres is almost beyond belief. Yet, Keynesians and Marxists, Curriculum Planners and Free Schoolers, Chinese and Americans, are all convinced that *homo* is *educandus*, that his well-being — nay, existence — depends on services from an educational sphere.

It is precisely this well-knit assumption of an educational sphere that becomes the subject of the research on education I would recommend, but only as part of a wider research on the process by which economics, politics, wage-labor, and domestic serfdom came into being. And this is the moment for such research, because the orthodox members of the cloister have lost the innocence of their convictions, while the heterodox have not yet found their new paradigm outside. The character of the approaching paradigm change is not yet clear, for the educational community is at a stage similar to that of astronomy at the Renaissance.

One of the principal figures in the development of astronomy at that time was Copernicus (1473–1543). He is one of the most popular examples cited when people write on paradigm changes in world views. In the literature, one finds an enormous appreciation of the importance of his *De revolutionibus coelorum*. All testify to his undoubted worth as a mathematical astronomer. But de Solla Price challenged this view. He actually believed it to be a dangerous myth. Since similar myths now envelope some anti-school prophets, I shall comment on Copernicus and his influence.

Importantly, he reopened the question of the earth's mobility. And he showed that no mathematical damage was incurred by assuming that it rotated around its axis. In a sense, he did go back to the Pythagorean position that the sun is at the center of the planetary orbs. Mathematically, he was the first to create a planetary system. All his predecessors had dealt with each planet separately; he integrated them. But he did not differ in method or in basic assumptions from Ptolemy. His demonstrations are derived from the so-called *Almagest*, and he accepted the existence of heavenly spheres. In terms of received knowledge, he admitted even more. He prided himself for having philosophically restored a strictly uniform circular motion to the heavenly bodies. However, this necessitated the positing of more circles than Ptolemy in order to avoid the use of eccentrics.

It can be argued that Copernicus did replace the potential crystal spheres that Dante — or, before him, Mohammed of the Ladder-Book — could visit by making planets move along prosaic spherical sections. But these neither he nor the young Kepler would think of renouncing. These men could not bring themselves to believe that there is not a natural difference between the movement of the heavens, which is perfect, and that of the sublunar, that is, sinful sphere. Perhaps for this reason the Inquisition did not bother them at all. But in 1600, Giordano Bruno was burned at the stake. Bruno, like the young Kepler, was influenced by Copernicus. But unlike him, he was not an observer of nature, nor did he know any mathematics. Probably wrongly, he imputed to Copernicus the power to prove that the universe is immense, peopled by innumerable stars, and uniform throughout in its nature. With this opinion, he was suggesting that one could think about the universe without spheres — and that led him to the stake.

But Bruno's relationship to astronomy is somewhat akin to that of the outsider in the educational debate today. Therefore, he is of no direct interest in speaking about research on education. Before Kepler, and with the one exception of Bruno, the sky of common sense was also that of philosophical cosmology and mathematical astronomy. The common subject, however, was not the stars themselves, but rather the spheres that carried the planets and the empyrean. The common interest lay in the perfectly circular movements of transparent concentric material realities of a special kind. Each such sphere carried a planet, was generated by it, and was named after the star. The star in turn indicated the influence that the sphere exercised in the world. Copernicus was a heavenly reformer, a rearranger of these spheres. He cannot serve as an example for educators.

In his day, Tycho Brahe (1546–1601) was the foremost observer of the heavens. Coming from a powerful Danish family, he was born when Copernicus died and, two years before his own death in 1601, accepted the young Kepler as an apprentice. During his lifetime, Brahe substantially corrected the accepted value of nearly every astronomical quantity. He was the first to allow for the refraction of the atmosphere, to introduce methods of correcting instrumental error, to suggest correctly the nature of a nova, to map the location of more than 7,000 fixed stars. As a practical astonomer, he surpassed all before him and, like them, he still looked at the sky with the naked eye alone.

Kepler approached him to learn because he felt that only Brahe could teach him the observational skills necessary to prove Copernicus correct. But from the beginning of the apprenticeship, Brahe strongly dissuaded Kepler from undertaking such a foolish project. Again, Brahe was the first to point out that the mathematical changes introduced by Copernicus were on the whole such that they increased enormously both the complexity of the calculation and the heavenly mechanism without increasing the accuracy of prediction for the location of stars. Dissatisfied with both Ptolemy and Copernicus, Brahe designed a third system, constructed on a middle ground between Ptolemaic and Copernican assumptions. He retained the immobility of the earth, but the other planets were made to revolve around the sun. The latter, with these planets, annually circuited the earth. In addition, all planets performed a diurnal rotation with the sphere of fixed stars. His correct claim, that this system was more elegant and simpler mathematically than that of Copernicus, indicates the monstrous complexity of the Copernicus system. Experimentally, none of the three systems could be verified. Due to their constant improvement, the Ptolemaic predictions possessed an edge. Pascal was correct in believing that only because of a cosmological prejudice could one possibly choose among the three. Instruments to observe the parallax of fixed stars became available only three centuries later.

When Brahe died, Kepler edited his monumental catalog of the stars. Then he began to see the point on which all three of his great predecessors — Ptolemy, Copernicus, and Brahe — were wrong: none of them could conceive of heavenly movements detached from heavenly spheres. Kepler did not attempt to replace the spheres with something else; he simply eliminated them.

Johannes Kepler (1571–1630) had a poetic and critical mind. Already as a student, in 1593 (a hundred years after the first return of Columbus), he had written out a series of speculations derived from Maestline's attempts to estimate the elevations on the lunar surface by measuring, in Tübingen, the shadows on the moon; a technique the ancient Greeks had already tried to use. During the summer of 1609, he wrote out a plan for landing on the moon, earth's closest neighbor in the sky. Kepler mentioned this project, never before conceived in scientific literature, in a letter to Galileo Galilei (April 19, 1610). He confided to his Italian friend:

> Last summer, the manuscript begun in 1593 has been expanded into a complete geography of the moon . . . who would have believed that a huge ocean could be crossed more peacefully and safely than the narrow expanse of the Adriatic, the Baltic Sea or the English Channel. . .? Provide ship or sail adapted to the heavenly breezes, and there will be some who will not fear even that void . . . so for those who will come shortly to attempt this journey, let us establish the astronomy: Galileo, you, that of Jupiter, and I that of the moon.

As Bruno had done by reasoning on general principles, so Kepler, concerned with ordering his observations, replaced a mechanism of spheres by heavenly bodies following their orbits. Voyaging from earth to other planets of the sun thus became a reasonable subject for intellectual speculation in 1609. Mundus became a new Cosmos interpreted by a new set of myths. Kepler confided his transgression of the 'spheric taboo' to a private diary written in the form of a dream. Through an indiscretion, some pages of this manuscript became known and led to the arrest of Kepler's mother and her confrontation with the instruments of torture, an experience from which she soon died. The *Somnium* was published two years after Kepler's death.

I am under the impression that the educational debate, no matter how radical, is still only concerned with a rearrangement of social spheres on the model of pre-Kepler stargazers. Correct observations on shared imagery and shared competence are still used, like those of Brahe, to fit a redundant paradigm. Discussion ranges, and research moves about the convenience or the necessity to redefine, to relate, to develop, or to appropriately add new epicycles within this one sphere. And when such educational policy alternatives pretend to be fundamental, the relationship of the educational to the other spheres takes prominence as an issue. Should production or politics be at the center of the social system? Or should the two be related in a more complex way, perhaps on the model of Tycho Brahe? Should we prefer an all-encompassing system of spheres on the Copernican model? Or is it better to muddle through without an overall system, but relying on the proven approximations that Al Shatir's eccentrics and epicycles permitted one to calculate, even though such a theory deals with only one Ptolemaic planet at a time? Shall the school system remain at the center? Or shall school be but one adjunct to the education that goes on, for example, in a Chinese commune? How shall we rank the different tools of education? Or how shall we relate the spheres of education, health, welfare, research, finance, economics, politics? I think that research on the model of Copernicus is not what we need in education.

Following Kepler's example, we now need to recognize that the educational sphere is a construct analogous to the sphere of Mercury, and that the need of humans to be educated can be compared with the need of humans to live at the static center of the universe. This educational construct is mapped by an ideology that brought into being our convictions about *homo educandus*. The construct is socially articulated by a specific set of institutions, for which *Alma Mater Ecclesia* is the prototype. It is implanted into the world view of each individual by a double experience: first, by the latent curriculum of all educational programs, through which vernacular learning is inevitably debased and, second, through life in the opaque, passive, and paralyzing lifestyle that professional control over the definition and satisfaction of needs inevitably fosters. Finally, the construct of the educational sphere is zealously guarded by the various bodies of educators who identify educational needs in terms of problems for which they alone possess the social mission to find institutional solutions in and out of schools.

This construct of an educational sphere is thoroughly consistent with other similar constructs, especially the spheres of economics and politics. The process through which each of these spheres has been disembedded to the point of achieving a radical monopoly that paralyzes its corresponding vernacular homolog can be studied separately for each one. But research on the educational sphere can claim a certain priority. Studying the process through which this sphere, in its ideological construction and in the degradation and replacement of vernacular languages by taught mother tongue after the invention of the loudspeaker, permits unique insights into the analogous elements that went into the constitution of other social spheres. Education as a subject matter and as a discipline has been defined by the construct and constrained by its basic assumptions up to now. This cannot be otherwise for research *in* education. But research on the relations of the educational domain to the global ideology of a society, together with the history of these relations, constitutes the kind of study which ought to be called research *on* education.

The History of *Homo Educandus*

Opening Speech at the Plenum of the
5th World Congress of the World Council of
Comparative Education Societies
Sorbonne, Paris, July 1984

Monsieur Debeauvais, thank you for the invitation to
address this assembly. My lecture will take the form of a
plea. I plead for research on the history of *homo educandus*.
The object of such a history is the social construction of *homo
educandus* and of the societal context within which his learning constitutes a process of personal enrichment with values
that are assumed to be scarce. The organization of society in
view of a human being in need of information and program-
ming must be understood as a neglected aspect in the history
of *homo œconomicus*.

I conceive of the social history of *homo educandus* as the
opposite of the *history of education*. The history of *homo
educandus* deals with the emergence of a social reality within
which 'education' is perceived as a basic human need. Some
of its elements take shape in Greek antiquity where the
invention of the full alphabet first allowed the detachment of
knowledge from the speaker. Without this alphabetic technique to fix a text and transmit an original, neither the
literature nor the science with which education deals can be
imagined. Other key elements that are presuppositions for
education take shape between Alcuin and Albert the Great.
Because only at the time of Alcuin are words first visually
separated from each other, and the text becomes visible to
the eye.

From then on it was possible to grasp the meaning of a text by looking at it, instead of pronouncing the words to make them understandable to the ear. Without this visualization of the text, there is no idea of 'knowledge' that is laid down and deposited in books, of knowledge that can be reproduced and communicated.

Sixty years ago Milman Parry introduced the distinction between orality and literacy into the study of epos and literature. His pupils have spelled out the importance of this detachment of language from the individual's speech for the constitution of a new kind of truth. But their insights have not touched the core of educational theory, notwithstanding the great efforts made by Walter Ong and Jack Goody.

Even less has the importance of word division in the earlier Middle Ages been recognized in its importance to the 'truth' the educationalist presupposes. Only word division made it possible to copy texts by sight and, what is more important, to verify the textual identity of two books, thus conceiving the idea that an absolutely identical knowledge exists somewhere behind two individual copies. Even less than Milman Parry's insights, has this touched education, except indirectly through the recuperation of Marshall McLuhan.

Without the historical evolution of this knowledge behind the text, John Amos Comenius (1592–1670) would have been unthinkable. It is this kind of truth which is needed by *homo educandus* whose history begins with him.

And so, at the time of Comenius the history of *homo educandus* begins, at least as a project and program: *omnibus, omnia omnino docendi*. With this intent to teach everybody everything thoroughly, the idea of *homo educandus* is defined. The new man is a being who ought to be taught whatever he should know or do.

The history of education stands in stark contrast to the history of *homo educandus*. The historian of education assumes the need for education as an a-historical given. The historian of education speaks as if, wherever there is human culture, there is also a knowledge stock that must be transmitted from generation to generation. He does not study the steps by which this need historically came into existence. He only studies how this need has been met by other societies in various times and in different ways.

The history of *homo educandus* must be distinguished from the history of education. But it must also not be reduced to the history of the interpretations that past societies have given to the pupil-teacher relationships which in their world were recognized as such. What meaning did Maimonides or Al Razi give to the teaching of young men? What meaning did *musiké* have for Greeks before and after writing became one of its subjects at the time when Plato was a child? What did *shastra* mean for Brahmins and *artes* for Hugh of Saint-Victor? These are questions that have been well studied by our colleagues from different disciplines: in the history of ideas, the *histoire des mentalités*, historical semantics and philosophy. But from all these the history of *homo educandus* must be distinguished: first, because its object bears no comparison with any social reality outside of Western tradition and, second, because its object is currently considered a historically non-problematic fact.

As a result, the history of *homo educandus* has been neglected. Our colleagues are unwilling to recognize that education is a concept *sui generis*, inconceivable in other societies and therefore inapplicable for a historical description of their past. Education, as the term is now used, means learning under the assumption that this learning is a prerequisite for all human activities while, at the same time, the opportunities for this learning are by their very nature in scarce supply. Thus understood, learning is an aspect of life which can be adequately distinguished from other aspects. Learning precedes, if not temporally at least logically, the competent execution of a socially expected task. Starting from this idea, which fits education, innumerable social features of other societies can be classified as occasions for 'learning.' Wherever the historian of education finds a poetry recital, a ritual, an apprenticeship, an organized game, he smells educational activity.

All textbooks on the history of education that I have consulted deal with their subject under the assumption that learning as a scare entity has always existed and only appeared in different guise and form. Through this assumption even Neanderthal man is subsumed into the sub-species of *homo educandus*, and his transition to neolithic culture ascribed to more competent teaching how to split flint. Pedagogues are so anxious to prove their own legitimate descent from Socrates, Varro or Buddha, that for them the history of *homo educandus* has become a taboo. Economists have been faced with a similar taboo, but unlike educational theorists, they have tried to deal with it. In the late eighteenth century, they defined their science as the study of values under the assumption of their scarcity. Economics became the discipline dealing with the application of scarce means to alternate ends. As the concepts used by this discipline became more prestigious, economists too have tried to apply them to long past ages and very distant societies. In economics, however, right from the beginning, this practice, by which the past is homogenized to fit contemporary categories, has been challenged. In the first decade of our century, Elie Halévy demonstrated that social behavior regulated by utilitarian assumptions constitutes a radical break with any previously stated assumption about social relations. Thirty years later, Karl Polanyi focused on the emergence of markets in Greece, India, Mesopotamia. He documented the slow process by which a formal economy comes to be disembedded, but only in a certain society: social interactions based on the assumption of scarcity then appear, and for a long period remain limited to a very precise and narrow domain. By his teaching, Polanyi laid the foundation for the historical study of scarcity. Louis Dumont, more recently, has carefully described how, from Mandeville to Marx, a perception of human nature that fits the perception of scarcity came into being. He calls this construct of the human — man dependent on the use of and acquisition of scarce means — *homo oeconomicus*. I want to plead for analogous studies on the emergence of *homo educandus*.

The recognition of *homo oeconomicus* as a modern social construction has made it possible to understand better what traditional cultures are. All known traditional cultures can be conceived as meaningful configurations that have as their principal purpose the repression of those conditions under which scarcity could become dominant in social relations. Such cultures enforce rules of behavior that obviate the appearance of scarcity, and therefore undercut envy and the fear of it. A clear and simple exposition of this has been made by Muchembled and Dupuy. No doubt, some cultures become so organized that they tolerate enclaves within which the assumption of scarcity can determine new social mechanisms: they allow spaces in which peddlers and hucksters, certain Sikhs, Jews or Chinese, sophists and medicine-men, can sell their skills at the going price. But the tolerance of such behavior in outsiders only underlines that it is perceived as immoral if it were pursued by the insider of the culture. The resistance to the spread of the regime of scarcity throughout society at large is a common feature that distinguishes the human condition from the regime of scarcity that you, Monsieur Debeauvais, have so aptly called: 'L'univers concentrationnaire.'

I am not saying that the recognition of scarcity as a social construction by economic historians and anthropologists has shaped industrial society, or that it has significantly affected economic thought. Alternative economics have barely been washed by it. However, the recognition of traditional culture as a remedy to the spread of scarcity and envy has laid the foundations for new theoretical departures and a new realism in the history of cultures and mentalities. What I plead for is an analogous attempt by those of us whose bread and butter is education. Once we recognize that the fundamental concepts with which we operate — educational needs, learning, scarce resources, etc. — correspond to a paradigm which is far from natural, the way to a history of *homo educandus* will be opened.

For two distinct reasons it is important that researchers in comparative education recognize that 'learning under the assumption of scarce opportunities' constitutes an incomparable feature of our unique kind of world. First, this would allow comparatists to limit their research to phenomena that do have common phenomenological features. This self-limitation would make the discipline into a more legitimate undertaking. Second, the recognition that the discipline deals with an odd, modern social phenomenon would make it possible to engage in disciplined comparisons between education and other social features that are heteronomous to education and, therefore, cannot be reduced to it. If this were done, comparative education could become one of the rare fields that attempts to clarify one of the least recognized and most characteristic aspects of our age: the survival, even at the heart of highly developed societies, of fantasies, behavioral rules and patterns of action that have successfully resisted colonization by the regime of scarcity. I expect that even though most of you come from education, many of you still know that you have never learned to walk or breathe.

Taught Mother Tongue

Prepared for a meeting on 'The Need for
New Terminology to deal with "Mother Tongues" ',
held at the Central Institute of Indian Languages.
The lecture was given to honor Prof. D.P. Pattanayak
Mysore, India, 1978

Language has become expensive. As language teaching has become a job, a lot of money is spent on the task. Words are one of the two largest categories of marketed values that make up the GNP. Money is spent to decide what shall be said, who shall say it, how, and when, and what kind of people should be reached by the utterance. The higher the cost of each uttered word, the more effort has gone into making it echo. In schools people learn to speak as they should. Money is spent to make the poor speak more like the wealthy, the sick more like the healthy, and the black more like the white. We spend money to improve, correct, enrich, and update the language of kids and that of their teachers. We spend more on the professional jargons that are taught in college, and still more in high schools to give each teenager a smattering of these languages: just enough to make them feel dependent on the psychologist, druggist, or librarian who is fluent in some special kind of English. We first spend money to make people as exclusively monolingual in standard, educated colloquial, and then — usually with little success — we try to teach them a minority dialect or a foreign tongue. Most of what goes on in the name of education is really language instruction, but education is by no means the sole public enterprise in which the ear and the tongue are groomed: administrators and entertainers, admen and news-men form large interest groups, each fighting for their slice of the language pie. I do not really know how much is spent in the United States to make words.

Energy accounting was almost unthinkable only ten years ago. It has now become an established practice. Today — but really only since a couple of years ago — you can easily look up how many BTUs or other energy units have gone into growing, harvesting, packaging, transporting, and mer-chandising one edible calorie of bread. The difference is enormous between the bread that is grown and eaten in a village of Greece and the bread sold by the A&P; about 40 times more energy goes into the latter. About 500 times more energy units went into building one cubic foot of St Cather-ine's College in Oxford in the sixties than was needed to build one cubic foot of the Bodleian Library which stands next door, and which I like much more. Information of this kind was available ten years ago, but nobody felt like tabulating it, and it made only a few people think. Today it is available, and very soon will change people's outlook on the need for fuels. It would now be interesting to know what language accounting would look like. The linguistic analysis of contemporary language is certainly not complete unless, for each group of speakers, we know the amount of money that was spent on the speech of each person. Just as social energy accounts are only approximate and permit — at best — identifying the orders of magnitude within which the relative values are to be found, so language accounting would provide us with data on the relative prevalence of taught language in a population — which would be sufficient for the argument that I would like to make.

The mere per capita expenditure on the language of a group of speakers would, of course, not tell us enough. Taught language comes in a vast range of qualities. The poor, for instance, are much more blared at than the rich, who can buy tutoring and, what is more precious, silence. Each paid word that is addressed to the rich costs, per capita, much more than each word addressed to the poor. Watts are more democratic than words. Yet, even without the more detailed language-economics on which I would like to draw, I can estimate that the dollars spent for fuel imports to the United States pale before those that are now expended on American speech. The language of rich nations is incredibly spongy and absorbs huge investments. Rising expenditures for tax collection, administration, theater, and other forms of costly language have always been a mark of high civilization, especially in urban life. But these fluctuations in expenditures for language (or fuel) were traditionally of a different kind, incomparable with the capitalization of language today. Even today, in poor countries, people still speak to each other, though their language has never been capitalized except, perhaps, among a tiny élite. What is the difference between the everyday speech groups whose language has received — absorbed? resisted? reacted to? suffered? enjoyed? — huge investments and the speech of people whose language has remained outside the market? I want to compare these two worlds of language, but focus my curiosity on just one issue that arises in this context: does the structure of the language itself change with the rate of investment? If so, are these changes such that all languages that absorb funds would show changes that go in the same direction? In my introductory discussion of the subject I may not be able to give you enough arguments to make both claims appear very probable and to convince you that structurally oriented language economics are worth exploring.

Taught everyday language is without precedent in preindustrial cultures. The current dependence on paid teachers and on models of *ordinary* speech is just as much a unique characteristic of industrial economies as is our dependence on fossil fuels. Both language and energy have only in our generation been recognized as worldwide needs that — for all people — must be satisfied by planned, programmed intervention. Traditional cultures subsisted on sunshine that was captured mostly through agriculture: the hoe, the ditch, the yoke were common; large sails or waterwheels were known but rare. Cultures that lived mostly on the sun subsisted basically on vernacular language that was absorbed by each group through its own roots. Just as power was drawn from nature mostly by tools that increased the skill of fingers and the power of arms and legs, so language was drawn from the cultural environment through the encounter with people, each of whom one could smell and touch, love and hate. Taught tongues were rare, like sails and mills. In most cultures we know, speech overcame man.

The majority in poor countries, even today, learn to speak without any paid tutorship; and they learn to speak in a way that in no way compares with the self-conscious, self-important, colorless mumbling that, after a long stay in villages of South America and Southeast Asia, surprised me again during my last visit to American campuses. For people who cannot hear the difference, I feel only contempt that I try hard to transform into sorrow for their tone-deafness. But what else shall I expect from people who are not brought up on mother's breast but on formulas: Nestlé if they are from poor families, and a formula prepared under the nose of Ralph Nader if they are born among the enlightened rich, or if they are foundlings whom the élite tutor in its institutions. For people trained to choose among packaged formulas, mother's breast appears as one more option. In the same way, for people who learned every language they know from somebody they believe to be their teacher, untutored vernacular seems just like another less-developed model among many.

But this is simply not so: language that is exempt from rational tutorship is a different kind of social phenomenon than language that is taught. Where untutored language is the predominant marker of a shared world, a sense of shared power within the group exists that cannot be duplicated by language that is delivered. One of the first ways this difference shows is in a sense of power over language itself — over its acquisition. The poor in non-industrial countries all over the world, even today, are polyglot. My friend the goldsmith of Timbuktu speaks Songhay at home, listens to Banbara on the radio, devotedly and with some understanding says his prayers five times a day in Arabic, gets along in two trade languages on the souk, converses in passable

French that he has picked up in the army — and none of those languages was formally taught him. Communities in which monolingual people prevail are rare except in three kinds of settings: in tribal communities that have not really experienced the late neolithic period, in communities that have experienced certain intense forms of discrimination, and among the citizens of nation-states that for several generations have enjoyed the benefits of compulsory schooling. To take it for granted that most people are monolingual is typical of the members of the middle class. Admiration for the polyglot unfailingly exposes the social climber.

Throughout history, untutored language was prevalent, but it was hardly ever the only kind of language known. Just as, in traditional cultures, some energy was captured through windmills and canals, and those who had large boats or those who had cornered the right spot on the brook could use their tool for a net transfer of power to their own advantage, so some people have always used a taught language to corner some privilege. But such additional codes remained either rare and special, or served very narrow purposes. The ordinary language, the vernacular, but also the trade idiom, the language of prayer, the craft jargon, and the language of basic accounts, was learned on the side, as part of everyday life. Of course, Latin or Sanskrit were sometimes formally taught to the priest; a court language, such as Frankish, Persian, or Turkish, was taught to him who wanted to become a scribe; neophites were formally initiated into the language of astronomy, alchemy, or late masonry. And, of course, the knowledge of such formally taught language raised a man above others, like the saddle of a horse. Quite frequently, in fact, the process of formal initiation did not teach a new language skill, but exempted the initiate from the taboo that forbade others to use certain words. Male initiation into the languages of the hunt and of ritual intercourse is probably the most widespread example of such a ritual of selective language 'de-tabooing.' But, no matter how much or how little language was taught, the taught language rarely rubbed off on vernacular speech. Neither the existence of some language teaching at all times nor the spread of some language through professional preachers or comedians weakens my key point: outside of those societies that we now call 'modern European,' no attempt was made to impose on entire populations an everyday language that would be subject to the control of paid teachers or announcers. Everyday language, until recently, was nowhere the product of design, it was nowhere paid for and delivered like a commodity. And while every historian who deals with the origin of nation-states pays attention to commodities, economists generally overlook language.

I want to contrast taught colloquial and vernacular speech, costly language and that which comes at no cost. I call the first 'taught colloquial' because, as we shall see, 'mother tongue' is fraught with tricky implications. 'Everyday language' might do, but is less precise, and most other terms that I shall occasionally use caricature one of the aspects of tutored language. For the opposite, I use the term 'vernacular' because I have nothing better. Vernacular comes from an Indo-Germanic root that implies 'rootedness' or 'abode.' It is a Latin word used in classical times for whatever was homebred, homespun, homegrown, homemade — be it a slave or a child, food or dress, animal, opinion, or a joke. The term was picked up by Varro to designate a distinction in language. Varro picked 'vernacular' to designate language that is grown on the speaker's own grounds as opposed to that which is planted there by others. Varro was a learned man, the most learned Roman according to the great teacher Quintillian, librarian to Caesar and then to Augustus, with considerable influence on the Middle Ages. So 'vernacular' came into English in just that one, restricted sense in which Varro had adopted it. I would now like to resuscitate some of its old breath. Just now we need a simple, straightforward word to designate the fruit of activities in which people engage when they are not motivated by considerations of exchange, a word that would designate non-market-related activities by which people do things and make do — wants to which, in the process of satisfying them, they also give concrete shape. 'Vernacular' seems a good old word that might be acceptable to many contemporaries for this usage. I know that there are technical words available to designate the satisfaction of those needs that economists do not or cannot measure: 'social production' as opposed to 'economic production'; the generation of 'use values' or 'mere use values,' as opposed to the production of 'commodities'; 'household economics' as opposed to the economics of the 'market.' But these terms are all specialized, tainted with some ideological prejudice, and they often limp. We need a simple adjective to designate those values that we want to defend from measurement and manipulation by Chicago boys or socialist commissars, and that adjective ought to be broad enough to fit food and language, childbirth and infant-rearing, without implying a 'private' activity or a backward procedure. By speaking about *vernacular language* I am trying to bring into discussion the existence of a *vernacular mode of being and doing* that extends to all aspects of life.

Before I can go on in my argument, I will have to clarify one more distinction. When I oppose taught language to the vernacular, I draw a line of demarcation somewhere else than linguists do when they distinguish between the high language of an élite and the dialect spoken in lower classes; somewhere else than that other frontier that allows us to distinguish between regional and supra-regional language; and, again, somewhere else than the demarcation line between the language of the illiterate and that of the literate. No matter how restricted within geographic boundaries, no matter how distinctive for a social level, no matter how specialized for one sex role or one caste, language can be either 'vernacular' (in the sense in which I use the term) or 'taught.' Elite language, second language, trade language, and local language are nothing new, but for each the *taught* variety that comes as a commodity is entirely new. I am not speaking now in detail about varieties of taught language, but I am focusing on taught everyday language, taught colloquial — which usually is taught *standard* colloquial. In all of recorded history, one among several mutually understandable dialects has tended towards predominance in a given region. This kind of predominant dialect was often

accepted as the standard form, that form which was written
— and that form which, earlier than others, was taught. This
dialect generally predominated because of the prestige of its
speakers. Most of the time it did not spread because it was
taught; it diffused by a much more complex and subtle
process. Midland English became the second, common style
in which people born into any English dialect could also
speak their own language, just as Bahasa Malayu became
the national tongue of Indonesia. Since both those language-
diffusions took place in rather modern times, we might
suspect that intentional teaching had something to do with
the process. For Urdu, which the Moghul soldiery spread
over the Indian subcontinent, teaching has hardly anything
to do with the sudden spread.

No doubt, the dominant position of élite or standard
language varieties everywhere was bolstered by writing, and
even more by printing. Printing enormously enhanced the
colonizing power of élite language. But to say that because
printing has been invented, élite language is destined to
supplant all vernacular varieties is to put the cart before the
horse; it's like saying that after the invention of the atom
bomb, only superpowers shall be sovereign. In fact, the
editing, printing, publishing, and distribution of printed
matter incorporated increasingly those technical procedures
that favor centralization and the colonization of vernacular
forms by the printed standard. But this monopoly of centralized procedures over technical innovations is no argument
that printing technique could not increasingly be used to
give written expression a new vitality and new literary
opportunities to thousands of vernacular forms. The fact that
printing was used for the imposition of standard colloquials
does not mean that written language will always be a taught
form.

Vernacular spreads by practical use; it is learned from
people who mean what they say and who say what they
mean to the person for whom what they say is meant. This is
not so in taught language. In the case of taught language, the
key model is not a person that I care for or dislike, but a
professional speaker. Taught colloquial is modeled by some-

body who does not say what he means, but who recites what others have contrived. Taught colloquial is the language of the announcer who follows the script that an editor was told by a publicist that a committee had decided should be said. Taught language is the dead, impersonal rhetoric of people paid to declaim with phony conviction texts composed by others. People who speak taught language imitate the announcer of news, the actor of gags, the instructor who follows the textbooks, the songster of engineered rhymes, or the ghost-written president. This language is not meant to be used when I say something to your *face*. The language of the media always seeks the appropriate audience-profile that has been chosen by the boss of the program. While the vernacular is engendered in the learner by his presence at the intercourse between people who say something to each other face to face, taught language is learned from speakers whose assigned job is gab.

Of course, language would be totally inhuman if it were totally taught. That is what Humboldt meant when he said that real language is that speech which can only be fostered, never taught like mathematics. Only machines can communicate without any reference to vernacular roots. Their chatter in New York now takes up almost three quarters of the lines that the telephone company operates under a franchise that guarantees free intercourse to people. This is an obvious perversion of a public channel. But even more embarrassing than this abuse of a forum of free speech by robots is the incidence of robot-like stock phrases in the remaining part in which people address each other. A growing percentage of personal utterances has become predictable, not only in content but also in style. Language is degraded to 'communication' as if it were nothing but the human variety of an exchange that also goes on between bees, whales and computers. No doubt, a vernacular component always survives; all I say is that it withers. The American colloquial has become a composite made up of two kinds of language: a commodity-like, taught uniquack, and an impoverished vernacular that tries to survive. Modern French and German have gone the same way, though with one difference: they have absorbed English terms to the point that certain standard exchanges in French or German that I have overheard in European drugstores and offices have all the formal characteristics of pidgin.

A resistance that sometimes becomes as strong as a sacred taboo guards the recognition of the difference with which we are dealing here: the difference between capitalized language and vernaculars that come at no economically measurable cost. It is the same kind of inhibition that makes it difficult for those who are brought up within the industrial system to sense the fundamental distinction between nurturing at the breast and feeding by bottle; or the difference between the pupil and the autodidact; or the difference between a mile moved on my own and a passenger mile; or the difference between housing as an activity and housing as a commodity — all things about which I have spoken in the past. While anyone would probably admit that there is a huge difference in taste, meaning, and value between a homecooked meal and a TV dinner, the discussion of this difference among people like us can be easily blocked. The people present at a meeting like this are all people who are committed to equal rights, equity, the service of the poor. They know how many mothers have no milk in their breasts, how many children in the South Bronx suffer protein deficiencies, how many Mexicans are crippled by lack of basic foods. As soon as I raise the distinction between vernacular values and those that can be economically measured and therefore administered, some protector of the poor will jump up and tell me that I am avoiding the critical issue by giving importance to niceties. I distinguish between transportation and transit by metabolic power, between vernacular and taught colloquial, between homemade food and packaged nutrition. Now, are not the distances covered on foot and by wheel, the terms used in learned and in taught language, and the calories ingested in the two kinds of food the same? No doubt they are, but this makes each of the two activities comparable only in a narrow, non-social sense. The difference between the vernacular movement, word or food and that which is overwhelmingly a commodity goes much deeper: the value of the vernacular is to a large measure determined by him who engenders it; the need for the commodity is determined and shaped for the consumer by the *producer* who defines its value. What makes the world *modern* is a replacement of vernacular values by commodities, which — to be attractive — must deny the essential value of the aspect that, in this process, is lost.

People who feel like modern men experience basic needs that correlate to commodities rather than to vernacular activities. Technologies that fit into this kind of world are those that apply scientific progress to commodity production rather than to the enlargement of vernacular competence. The use of writing and printing at the service of the standard colloquial in preference to its use for the expansion of the vernacular reflects this deeply ingrained prejudice. What makes the work process modern is the increased intensity with which human activity is managed and planned, and the decreased significance that those activities can claim for themselves, rather than for exchange on the market. In his essay 'The Limits to Satisfaction,' William Leiss argues this point. I will incorporate here some of his argument, because later I would like to show how the process he describes has affected language since the rise of Europe as an ideal. Leiss argues that the radical transformation of individual wants in the process of industrialization is the hidden complement of the attempt to dominate nature. This attempt to dominate nature has, since the seventeenth century, progressively shaped and branded every aspect of public pursuits in Western societies. Nature was increasingly interpreted as the source from which a social production process is fed: an enterprise that is undertaken for people rather than by them. 'Needs' designated, increasingly, rights to the output of this process rather than claims for the freedom and competence to survive. As the environment (which formerly was called 'nature') became ruthlessly exploited as a resource and as a trash can for those commodities that were being produced for the purpose of satisfying needs, human nature (which today is called human psychology) avenged itself. Man became needy. Today, the individual's feelings about his own needs are first associated with an increasing feeling of impotence: in a commodity-dominated environment, needs can no longer be satisfied without recourse to a store, a market. Each satisfaction that commodity-determined man experiences implies a component of frustrated self-reliance. It also implies an experience of isolation and a sense of disappointment about the persons that are close. The person that I can touch and cherish cannot give me what I need, cannot teach me how to make it, cannot show me how to do without it. Every satisfaction of a commodity-shaped need thus undermines further the experiences of self-reliance and of trust in others that are the warp and woof of any traditional culture. Leiss analyzes what happens when the number and the variety of goods and services grow, each of which is offered to the individual, each interpreted as a need, and each symbolically constituting a utility. The individual is forced to relearn how to need. His wants crumble into progressively smaller components. His wants lose their subjective coherence. The individual loses the ability to fit his need-fragments into a whole that would be meaningful to him. Needs are transformed from drives that orient creative action into disorienting lacks that call for professional service to synthesize demand. In this high-commodity setting, the adequate response to any commodity-determined need ceases to imply the satisfaction of the person. The person is understood as forever 'in need' of something. As needs become limitless, people become increasingly needy. Paradoxically, the more time and resources are expended on generating commodities *for the supposed satisfaction of needs*, the more shallow becomes each individual want, and the more indifferent to the specific form in which it shall be met. Beyond a very low threshold, through the replacement of vernacular forms of subsistence by commodity-shaped needs and the goods or services that fit them, the person becomes increasingly needy, teachable, and frustrated.

This analysis of the correlation between needs, commodities, and satisfaction provides an explanation for the limitless demand that economists and philosophers today tend to postulate, and for which empirical evidence seems not to be lacking. The social commitment to the replacement of vernacular activities by commodities is, in fact, at the core of today's world. On this ground alone, ours is a new kind of world, incomparable to any other. But as long as this trend subsists, ours is also a world in which the increase of supply of those kinds of things that teachers or fuel lines make will correspond to increasing frustration. In a world where 'enough' can be said only when nature ceases to function as pit or as trash can, the human being is oriented not towards satisfaction but towards grudging acquiescence.

Where shall we look for the roots of this inversion of values, for this transformation of human psychology in the pursuit of the domination of nature? To say that the roots of this inversion lie in the 'rise of capitalism' would be to take the symptom for the disease. Socialism that enshrines at its core the provision of goods and services to each one according to his or her needs is just as much dependent on the belief that needs correlate to commodities as any of those doctrines that socialists call 'capitalist.' The root of the inversion is much deeper. It is, of course, of a symbolic, religious nature, and demands an understanding of the past and the future of 'education,' the issue that has brought us together. If we examine when and how ordinary everyday language became teachable, we might gain some episodic insight into this event.

Nobody has ever proposed to teach the vernacular. That is, at least as I use the term, impossible and silly. But I can follow the idea that the colloquial is somehow teachable down into Carolingian times. It was then that, for the first time in history, it was discovered that there are certain basic needs, needs that are universal to mankind and that cry out for satisfaction in a standard fashion that cannot be met in a vernacular way. The discovery might be best associated with the Church reform that took place in the eighth century and in which the Scottish monk Alcuin, living a good part of his life as court philosopher to Charlemagne, played a prominent role. Up to that time, the Church had considered its ministers primarily as priests, that is, as persons selected and invested with special powers to meet communitary, public needs. They were needed to preach and to preside at functions. They were public officials analogous to those others through whom the state provided the defense of the commonweal against enemy and famine, or the administration of justice or public order and public works.

To call public servants of this kind 'service professionals' would be a double mistake, a silly anachronism. But then, from the eighth century on, the precursor of the service professional began to emerge: church-ministers who catered to the personal needs of parishioners, equipped with a theology that defined and established those needs. Priests slowly turned into pastors. The institutionally defined care of individual, the family and the community acquired unprecedented prominence. Thus, the bureaucratic provision of services that are postulated as a 'natural' need of all members of mankind takes shape long before the industrialization of the production of goods. Thirty-five years ago Lewis Mumford tried to make this point. When I first read his statement that the monastic reform of the ninth century created some of the basic assumptions on which the industrial system is founded, I had many reasons to reject this insight. In the meantime, though, I found a host of arguments — most of which Mumford seems not even to suspect — for rooting the ideologies of the industrial age in the Carolingian Renaissance. The idea that there is no salvation without *personal services* from the institutional church is one of these formerly unthinkable discoveries without which, again, our own age would be unthinkable. No doubt, it took 500 years of medieval theology to elaborate on this concept. Only by the end of the Middle Ages was the pastoral self-image of the Church fully rounded. Only during Vatican Council II, within our own generation, will the same Church that served as the prime model in the evolution of secular service organizations align itself explicitly with the image of its imitators. But what counts here, the concept that the clergy can define its own services as needs of human nature and make this service commodity into a necessity that cannot be foregone by any single human being without jeopardy to eternal life. This concept is of medieval origin. It is the foundation without which the contemporary service or welfare state would be inconceivable. Surprisingly little research has been done on the religious core concepts that fundamentally distinguish the industrial age from all other societies. The decline of the vernacular conception of Christian life in favor of one organized around pastoral care is a complex and drawn-out process that I mention here only because it constitutes a necessary background for the understanding of a similar shift in the understanding of language.

Three stages can be distinguished in the evolution of the vernacular into industrial uniquack — a term that James Reston first used when Univac was the only commercial computer. The first step is the appearance of the term 'mother tongue' and monkish tutorship over vernacular speech. The second is the transformation of mother tongue into national language under the auspices of grammarians. The third is the replacement of schooled and educated standard language based on written texts by our contemporary, medium-fed, high-cost idiom.

The terms and the concepts of mother tongue and mother country were both unknown until the High Middle Ages. The only classical people who conceived of their land as related to 'mother' were the early Cretans; memories of a matriarchal order still lingered in their culture. When Europe took shape as a political reality and as an idea, people spoke 'people's language,' the *sermo vulgaris*. '*Duits*' means precisely that. In patriarchally-minded Roman law, a person's vernacular was presumed to be his or her *patrius sermo* — the speech of the male head of the household. Each *sermo* or speech was also perceived as a language. Neither the early Greeks nor people in the early Middle Ages made our distinction between mutually understandable 'dialects' and distinct 'languages,' a distinction that people on the grassroots level of India equally do not yet make. During the last three decades I have had the opportunity to observe many hundreds of highly motivated and intelligent foreign academics seeking entrance to village life in South America and then in Southeast Asia. Again and again I was struck by the difficulty these people have, even when they are trained as social scientists, in understanding the lucid simplicity with which people can identify with one — or with several — forms of vernacular in a way in which only the exceptional poet can live a taught language with every one of his fibers. The vernacular was, in this sense, unproblematic up until the eleventh century. At that moment, quite suddenly, the term 'mother tongue' appears. It appears in the sermons of several monks from the Abbey of Gorz and marks the first attempt to make the choice of vernacular into a moral issue. The mother Abbey of Gorz in Lorraine, not far from Verdun, had been founded in the eighth century by Benedictines, over a church dedicated to St Gorgonius. During the ninth century the monastery decayed in a scandalous way. Three generations later, by the tenth century, the Abbey became the center of Germanic monastic reform; parallel, east of the Rhine, of the Cistercian reform Abbey of Cluny. Within two generations, 160 daughter abbeys, founded (or engendered) by Gorz were scattered all through the Germanic territory of the Holy Roman Empire. Gorz itself was located near the dividing line between Romance and Frankish vernaculars, and the monks from Gorz wanted to stop the challenge or advance of the competing monks from Cluny. They made language into an issue and a tool for their claim.

The monks of Gorz launched into language politics by attaching to the term 'language' a curious epithet, namely, 'mother' — an epithet that was ideologically charged at that time in a manner that is, again, difficult for us to grasp. The symbolic maternity of the Church, the universal maternity of the Virgin Mary, was central to the experience of personal life and of cosmic reality with an intensity that you can glean only by reading the original poetry of the time or by sitting quietly in front of one after another of the great statues representing Romanesque art. By coining the term 'mother tongue,' the monks of Gorz elevated the unwritten vulgate, vernacular '*Duits*'into something that could be honored, cherished, defended against defilement and otherwise treated as mother should be. Language was consecrated through its relation with maternity and, at the same time, maternity was alienated by one more step into a principle over which the male clergy could claim power. Mother was now honored and managed, cherished and used, protected in her purity and forged into a weapon, guarded against defilement and used as a shield. The professional pastorate, which today we would understand as a service profession, had made an important step in acquiring responsibilities in the performance of maternal functions.

From the Frankish of the eleventh century the term was translated into low Latin as *materna lingua* and thus spread throughout Europe, only to be rediscovered and retranslated into various forms of the vulgate in the early fifteenth century. With the concept of 'mother tongue,' of a supra-regional colloquial with highly charged emotional value and a broad audience, a condition was created that called for the invention of moveable type and print. Gutenberg made his invention when the language that he needed for its acceptance was ripe.

The next step in the mutation of the vernacular coincides with the development of a device by which the teaching of mother tongue could be taken over by men. The medieval preachers, poets, and Bible translators had only tried to consecrate, elevate, and endow with the nimbus of mystical maternity that language that they heard among the people. Now a new breed of secular clerics, formed by humanism, consciously used the vulgar as raw material for an engineering enterprise. The manual of specifications for correct sentences in the vernacular makes its appearance.

The publication of the first grammar in any modern European language was a solemn event, in late 1492. That year the Moor was driven from Granada, the Jews were expelled from Toledo, and the return of Columbus from his first voyage was expected any day. That year, Don Elio Antonio de Nebrija dedicated the first edition of his *Grammatica Castellana* to his Queen, Isabel la Católica. At the age of 19, Nebrija had gone to Italy, where Latin had least decayed and was best cultivated, to bring back to life in Spain the one language that as a young man he had considered worthy and that, in his opinion, had died in barbarian neglect in his home country. Hernán Núñez, a contemporary, compared him to Orpheus bringing back Euridice. For almost a generation he was in Salamanca, at the center of renewal of classical grammar and rhetoric. Now, in his fifty-second year, he finished his grammar of the spoken language and, shortly afterwards, the first dictionary that already contains a word from overseas: 'canoa-canoe,' which Columbus had in the meantime brought back with the first sample Indian.

As I said, Nebrija dedicated his grammar to Isabel, who was a very uncommon woman, too. In battle she dressed as a knight and at court surrounded herself with humanists who consistently treated her as an equal. Six months earlier, Nebrija had sent a draft of the book to the queen. For this draft she had expressed her gratitude and admiration for the author who had done for Castillian what, so far, had been done only for the languages of Rome and Greece. But with her appreciation she also expressed her perplexity. She was unable to understand to what use such a grammar could be put. Grammar was a teaching tool — and the vernacular was not something anybody could ever be taught. In her kingdoms, the queen insisted, every subject was destined by nature for a perfect dominion over his tongue. This royal sentence expresses a majestic principle of political linguistics. In the meantime, this sense of vernacular sovereignty has been largely administered away.

In the introduction to the first edition which was published in late 1492, Nebrija defends his undertaking by answering the queen. I have translated parts of his three-page argument, because any paraphrase would water it down:

> My illustrious Queen. Whenever I ponder over the tokens of the past that writing has preserved for us, I return to the same conclusion: language has forever been the mate of empire and always shall remain its comrade. Together they start, together they grow and flower, together they decline.

Please note the shift from 'mother' to 'mate'. He enunciated the new betrothal of *armas y letras* — the military and the university. Please note how the ever-changing patterns of vernacular speech may now be held up against a standard language that measures their improvement and their debasement.

> Castilian went through its infancy at the time of the judges . . . it waxed in strength under Alphonse the Wise who gathered laws and histories and who had many Arabic and Latin works translated.

Indeed, Alphonse X was the first European monarch who used his native tongue to insist that he was no longer a Latin king. His translators were mostly Jews, who preferred the vulgar tongue over the Church's Latin. Please note Nebrija's awareness that the standard language is strengthened as it is used for the writing of history, as a medium for translation and for the embodiment of laws.

> Thus our language followed our soldiers whom we sent abroad to rule. It spread to Arragon, to Navarra, and hence even to Italy. . . The scattered bits and pieces of Spain were thus gathered and joined into one single kingdom.

Note the role of the soldier who forges a new world and creates a new role for the cleric, the pastor educator.

> So far this language of Castile has been left by us loose and unruly and therefore, in just a few centuries, this language has changed beyond recognition. Comparing what we speak today with the language of 500 years ago, we notice a difference and diversity that could not be greater if these were two alien tongues.

Please note how in this sentence language and life are torn asunder. The language of Castile is treated as if, like Latin and Greek, it were already dead. Instead of the constantly evolving vernacular, Nebrija is referring to something totally different: timeless colloquial. He clearly reflects the split that has come into Western perception of time. The clock had come into the city, had been lifted onto a pedestal, had been made to rule the town. Real time, made up of equal pieces of equal length no matter if it was summer or winter, had first come to dictate the rhythm in the monastery and now began to order civic life. As a machine has governed time, grammar shall govern speech.

But let us go back to Nebrija:

> To avoid these variegated changes I have decided to . . . turn the Castilian language into an artifact so that whatever shall be henceforth written in this language shall be of one standard coinage that can outlast the times. Greek and Latin have been governed by art and thus have kept their uniformity throughout the ages. Unless the like of this be done for our language, in vain your Majesty's chroniclers . . . shall praise your deeds. Your labor will not outlast more than a few years and we shall continue to feed on Castilian translations of strange and foreign tales (about our own kings). Either your feats will fade with the language, or they will roam among aliens abroad, homeless without a dwelling in which they can settle.

Please note how Nebrija proposes to substitute for the vernacular a 'device,' an '*artificio*.' Unruly speech shall henceforth be substituted by standard coinage. Only 200 years earlier, Dante had still assumed that any language that had been learned and that is spoken according to a grammar could never come alive. Such language, according to Dante, could not but remain the device of schoolmen, of '*inventores grammaticae facultatis*.' Nebrija has a different perspective on power and rule. He wants to teach people the language of clerics, to tighten their speech and to subject their utterances to his rule. For Isabel the Queen, language was perceived as a domain. For her, the vernacular is the domain of the present, the utterance in which every speaker is sovereign. For Don Antonio the grammarian, language is a tool that serves, above all, the scribe. With a few words, he translates his 'dream of reason' into a monstrous ideology, the supposition on which, henceforth, the industrial system shall rise. Artifact shall substitute for autonomous subsistence; standard shall replace unruly variety; predictable outcomes shall remove the risk of surprise. He presses language into the service of fame — or more precisely, of a new kind of fame that is best called 'propaganda.'

> I want to lay the foundations of that dwelling in which your fame can settle. I want to do for my language what Zenodotos has done for Greek and Krates for Latin. No doubt, their betters have come after them. But to have been improved upon by their pupils does not detract from their, nay, from our, glory to be the originator of a necessary craft, just when its time had become ripe; and, may you trust me, no craft has ever come more timely than grammar for the Castilian tongue.

In only a few lines, Nebrija spells out the sales talk of the expert to his government that henceforth becomes standard:

> Majesty, you need the engineer, the inventor who knows how to make out of your people's speech, out of your people's lives, tools that befit your government and its pursuits. No doubt, believing in progress, I know that others will come who shall do better than I; others will build on the foundations that I lay. But, watch out, my lady, *you* cannot delay accepting my advice: 'This is the time. Our language has indeed just now reached a height, from which we must more fear that it slide than we can hope that it ever shall rise.'

Already, the expert is in a hurry. Already, he blackmails his patron with the 'now or never' that leads to so many modern policy decisions. The queen, according to Nebrija, needs the grammar now, because soon Columbus shall return.

> After your Majesty shall have placed her yoke unto many barbarians who speak outlandish tongues, by your victory these shall stand in new needs: in need for the laws that the victor owes to the vanquished and in need of the language that we bring. My

grammar shall serve to impart to them the Castilian tongue as we have taught Latin to our young.

We know well whose concept of language won out: language became one more tool managed by the professional lackey to power. Language was seen as an instrument to make people good, to make good people. Language became one of the major ingredients put by the hermetic alchemist into the formula by which new men were made to fit a new world. Mother tongue, as taught in the church and the classroom, replaced the vernacular that mother spoke. Mother tongue became a commodity centuries earlier than mother's milk. Men took charge of the '*educatio prolis*,' shaping Alma Mater as their social womb and breast. In the process, the sovereign subject became a citizen client. The domination of nature and the corresponding improvement of people became central public — supposedly secular — goals. '*Omnibus, omnia, omnino docendi ars*' — 'to teach everybody everything totally' — became the task of the educator, as John Amos Comenius spelled it out in the title of his book. The sovereign subject turned into a ward of the state. The doctrine about the need for primary education for the exercise of citizenship destroyed the autonomy of Isabel's subjects: she could tax her subjects, force them to statute labor or call them into the army; she could not attain the sovereign dignity of their tongue as every school teacher does.

The third mutation in the vernacular has happened under our eyes. Most people born before World War II, rich and poor alike, learned most of their first language either from persons who spoke to them, or from others whose exchanges they overheard. Few learned it from actors, preachers or teachers, unless that was the profession of their parents. Today, the inverse is the case. Language is fed to the young through channels to which they are hooked. What they learn is no more a vernacular that, by definition, we draw into us from roots, that we send out into a context in which we are anchored. The roots that serve for this purpose have become weak, dry and loose during the age of schooling and now, in the age of life-long education, they have mostly rotted away, like the roots of plants grown in hydroponics. The young and their linguists cannot even distinguish any more between the vernacular and the high-class slang that they take to be 'gutsy.' Language competence now, to a large degree, depends on sufficient supply of teaching.

The lack of personal sovereignty, of autonomy, appears clearly in the way people speak about teaching. At this very moment I am talking to you and, in another four minutes, I will be speaking with you, when the time for discussion will have come; but neither now, nor then, will I be teaching. I am arguing a point, presenting to you my opinions — perhaps I am even entertaining you. But I refuse to be pressed by you into your service as a teacher. Much less am I educating you. I do not want anything to do with that task for which nature has not provided me with the necessary organs. I have told you, perhaps, about some facts that had escaped you about the Abbey of Gorz or the court of the Catholic kings; but, believe me, it was done without any intent at shaping or trapping you for the sake of education. And I hope that I have convinced you that it is more than a terminological nicety when I insist that teaching is a very peculiar, always hierarchical, form that conversation in the vernacular sometimes takes. Unfortunately, many of our contemporaries cannot grasp this any more. Language has become for them a commodity, and the task of education that of training language producers by equipping them with a language stock.

A short while ago I was back in New York in an area that two decades ago I had known quite well: the South Bronx. I was there at the request of a young college teacher who is married to a colleague. This man wanted my signature on a petition for compensatory pre-kindergarten language training for the inhabitants of a slum. To overcome my resistance against this expansion of educational services, for a whole day he took me along on visits to brown, white, black and other so-called 'households.' I saw dozens of children in uninhabitable high-rise slums, exposed to all-day TV and radio, equally lost in landscape and in language. My colleague tried to convince me that I should sign the petition. And I tried to argue the right of these children for protection from education. We simply did not meet. And then in the evening, at dinner in my colleague's home, I suddenly understood why: this was no longer a man but a total teacher. In front of their own children, this couple stood '*in loco magistri.*' Their children had to grow up without parents — because these two adults, in every word which they addressed to their two sons and one daughter, were 'educating' them. And since they considered themselves very radical, off and on they made attempts at 'raising the consciousness' of their children. Conversation has turned for them into a form of marketing — of acquisition, production and sale. They have words, ideas, sentences; but they do not speak any more.

PART THREE

H₂O and the Waters of Forgetfulness

Lecture to the Dallas Institute
of Humanities and Culture
May 1984

I am told that for the last 70 years there have been citizens in Dallas who have urged the construction of a mid-city lake. The community expects this lake to water finance and fantasy, commerce and health. A commission is at work to explore the feasibility of such an artificial body of water downtown. Toward this study the Dallas Institute of Humanities and Culture would like to make a distinctive contribution: we are to reflect on the relationship between Water and Dreams, insofar as this bond is part of 'What makes a City Work.' Dreams have always shaped cities, and cities have always inspired dreams, and traditionally water has quickened them both. I have serious doubts that the water is left that can connect the two. Industrial society has turned H_2O into a substance with which the archetypal element of water cannot mix. My lecture, therefore, is divided into two parts. The first evokes the dream waters of Lethe, and the second introduces the history of flush. The conclusion comes back to the initial question about fantasy life among engineered things which have lost the elementary power to mirror the unfathomable waters of dreams.

In the city of Kassel a German baroque prince has built himself a castle surrounded by English gardens which solicit the waters to betray all they can tell. Water is not only meant to reveal itself to the eye and the touch, but to speak and sing in seventeen different registers. Thus dream waters mumble and ebb and swell and roar and trickle and splash and stream and dally, and they wash you and can carry you away. They can rain from above and well up from the depths: they can moisten or just wet. From all these wonders of water, I select its power to clean: Lethe's ability to wash off memories and H_2O's function to eliminate waste.

Dreams perform catharsis, which means that they clean, and dream waters can clean in several ways. The sprinkling with holy — *lustral* — water dissolves *miasma*; it quenches curses, dispels the pollution that lingers at certain places, can be poured on the hands, the head or the feet to wash off impurity, blood or guilt. But there is another catharsis which only the dark waters of Lethe perform: Lethe's waters detach those who cross them from memories and allow them to forget. Since I have only thirty minutes to speak to you, Lethe's catharsis is the only one I can address. This makes my question about the proposed city lake very narrow: can the soul's river of forgetfulness which flows into the social pool of remembrance reflect itself in the purified disinfectant that is metered, sewered and piped and then poured into an open-air reservoir downtown? Can the city child's dreams about 'letting go and forgetting' be watered by the liquid that comes from taps, showers and toilets? Can purified waste-water 'circulate' in fountains or lakes that mirror dreams?

The lustral waters of Lethe *flow*; they do not *circulate* like the blood and the money and the piped flush that swell the social imagination of the early industrial age. Already in 1616 William Harvey had announced to the London College of Physicians that blood circulates through the human body. It took Harvey's idea well over a century before it was generally accepted by practising physicians. In 1750 Dr Johannes Pelargius Storch, the authoritative creator of an eight-volume gynaecology, still could not accept the general validity of Harvey's theory. He accepted that blood might flow through the bodies of Englishmen and wash out their wastes; in his own patients, the women of lower Saxony, he observed the blood flowing and ebbing through the flesh. Storch understood what we now grapple to grasp: the fact that the re-definition of blood as a medium of circulation calls forth the social reconstruction of the body. The quivering and symbol-laden flesh and blood of tradition must be recast as a functional system of filters and conduits. By the end of the eighteenth century Harvey's theory was generally accepted in medicine. The conception of personal health based on the brisk circulation of blood fitted the mercantilist model of wealth — just before Adam Smith — based on the intensity of money circulation.

By the mid-nineteenth century several British architects began to speak about London according to this same paradigm and repeatedly recognized their debt to the 'immortal Harvey'. They conceived the city as a social body through which water must incessantly circulate, leaving it without pause as a carrier of dirt. Without interruption water must flow into the city to wash waste and sweat from it. The brisker this flow, the fewer the reservoirs that breed 'congenial pestilence,' the healthier the city will be. Unless water constantly flows into the city and is constantly pulled out through its sewers, the new city thus created by the imagination cannot but stagnate and rot. Just as Harvey had created something previously unimaginable, namely blood as a medium of circulation and thus the body of modern medicine, so Chadwick and Ward and their colleagues by the creation of flush invented the city as a place that needs to be constantly relieved of its remains. Like the body and the economy, the city could be henceforth visualized as a system of pipes.

The history of H_2O as the embodiment of archetypal water could be written in many ways. I here deal with the engineered degradation of the substance that makes it refractory, unfit to carry the metaphor we would like it to serve. All I can do here is to insist that 'water', unlike 'H_2O', is a historical construct which mirrors — for better or for worse — the fluid element of the soul, and that the H_2O-bound water of social imagination can be very far out of tune with the water for which we long in our dreams. Today's city water constantly crosses city limits: it comes in as a commodity and it goes out as a waste. In contrast, in all Indo-

Germanic myths, water itself is the limit. It separates this world from the other; it divides the world of those now living from the past one, or from the next. In the large family of Indo-Germanic myths the other world does not have one fixed location on the mental map: it may be located below the earth, on a mountain top, on an island, in the sky or in a cave. However, everywhere in this other world is a realm that lies beyond a body of water: beyond the ocean, on the other shore of a bay. To reach it, a river must be crossed: here you are ferried, there you must wade. But in all myths this way that leads through the waters, on the other side leads to a spring, and the river that you have crossed also feeds this otherworldly well.

Bruce Lincoln has shown that Greek, Indic, Nordic and Celtic pilgrims on their way to the beyond all cross through the same funereal landscape designed according to the same mythical hydrology. The slow-flowing waters the traveller crosses are those of the river of forgetfulness. This river has the power to strip those who cross it of their memories. The sleepy beating of the head in the *threnos* with which the mourning women lull the heroes of Thebes into their last sleep reminds Aeschylus of the monotonous beat of the oars across the river Acheron. However, what the river has washed from those on their way to the beyond, is not destroyed: the traveller is only divested of the deeds by which he will be remembered. The river carries them to a spring where they bubble up like the sand at the bottom of a cosmic well to serve as drink for the elect: the singer, the dreamer, the seer, the wise. The water induces drunkenness of a sober kind 'sobriam ebriatatem.' Through these messengers who have returned from their dreams or journeys, a trickle of living water from the realm of the dead brings them back their memories for which they have no more need, but which are of immense value to the living. Thus the dead depend on the living much less than the living on the dead. What the river Lethe has washed from their feet, the throbbing well of Mnemosyne, returns to life.

When the sky still lay in the arms of Earth, when Uranus still shared his bed with 'broadhipped Gaya', the Titans came into existence. And, in this firstborn generation that preceded the Gods, there was Mnemosyne. She is too old, too archaic, to be the mother of Apollo, but she furnishes him, Maya's son, with a soul which always finds its way back to the source, which can never forget. Hermes-Apollo thus has two mothers, and this seems to make him into the God-guide. The hymn to Hermes calls her the Mother of Muses. Hesiod distinctly remembers her flowing hair when he describes her stretched out with Zeus engendering her daughters. She herself is the pool in which the Muse of Enthusiasm bathes, no less than the other daughter, Forget-fulness. This appearance of Mnemosyne among the Titans who precede the Gods is crucial in the history of our water. By being placed among the Titans, a cosmic element becomes the source of remembrance; the well of culture, the spring of a first kind of city — and water as the source of remembrance acquires the feature of woman.

However, this archaic well of oral tradition has no place in the classical cities. The classical cities of Greece and, above all Rome, are built around aqueducts piping water to fountains. Not the well feeding a pond, not the epical singer, but engineered jets of water and written texts consigned to books shape their flow of water and of words. No Greek city has preserved an altar or well dedicated to Mnemosyne. She is still invoked by literate poets who want to rub shoulders with Homer. But Mnemosyne is no more the source of sober intoxication. Her name now stands as a personification for the literate storehouse of memory which Plato knew would dry up remembrance as the throbbing source beyond the river of Forgetfulness, remembrance as the pool fed by the terminal river. Remembrance as the Titanic co-mother of Hermes is replaced by a new kind of memory, as written culture replaces oral, and legal the old customary order.

From the well to the jet, from the pond of remembrance to the sculpted fountain, from epic song to referenced memory, water as a social metaphor goes through a first profound transformation. The waters of oral culture that flowed beyond the shores of this world are turned into the most treasured provision with which a government can supply the city. Given the task, I would begin by writing the history of the changing shape and the meaning that the changing perception of water gives to the city. In such a history the fountains of Rome, the waterworks of Isphahan and the channels of Venice and Tenochtitlán would appear as extreme and rare creatures. The city built along a river, the city constructed around the well as if it were the navel, the city depending on rainwater from the roofs, would become ideal types among many. However, with rare exceptions, all cities into which water is brought on purpose from afar have had until recently one thing in common: what the aqueduct brings across the city line is absorbed by the soil of the city. The idea that the water that is piped into the city must leave it by its sewers did not become a guiding principle for urban design until the steam engine was already a common sight. In the meantime, this idea has acquired the appearance of inevitability — even now when the sewer often leads into a treatment plant. What these plants produce and generate is further than ever from the water of dreams. The cities' need for a constant toilet has only tightened its hold on the planners' imagination. To loosen the spell of this social construct on our imagination I propose to study how this spell was cast.

The complaint that cities are dirty places goes back to antiquity. Even Rome with its nine hundred fountains was a dangerous place to walk. A special kind of petty magistrate sat under umbrellas on one corner of the forum: they heard and adjudicated complaints from people hurt by excrements thrown from windows. Medieval cities were cleaned by pigs. Dozens of ordinances survive which regulate the right of burghers to own pigs and feed them on public waste. The smell of tanneries was a cypher for hell. However, the perception of the city as a place that must be constantly deodorized by washing has a clearly defined origin in history: it appears at the time of the early Enlightenment. The new concern with scrubbing and cleaning is primarily directed toward the removal of features which are not so much visually ugly as objectionable in an olfactory sense. The whole city is now for the first time perceived as an evil-smelling place. The utopia of an odorless city is here first proposed. And, as far as I can judge, the new concern with the cities' odors reflects primarily a transformation of sense perception and not an increase of the air's saturation with gases having a characteristic smell.

The history of sense perception is not entirely new, but only recently have some historians begun to pay attention to the evolution in the sense of smell. It was Robert Mandrou who in 1961 first called attention to the primacy of touch, smell and hearing in pre-modern European cultures. This complex dark texture of sense-perception only slowly gave way to the 'enlightened' predominance of the eye that we take for granted. When a Ronsard or a Rabelais touches the lips of his love, he claims to derive his pleasure from taste and from smell. To write about the past perceptions of odors would be the supreme historical achievement: since odors leave no 'objective' trace whatsoever, the historian can know only how things were perceived. Last year, Alain Corbin made a first monographic attempt at describing the transformation of odor perception at the end of the *Ancien Régime*.

From my own experience I still know the traditional smell of cities. During two decades I have spent much of my time in city slums between Rio and Lima, Karachi and Benares. It took me a long time to overcome my inbred revulsion against the odor of human shit and stale urine that, with slight national variations, makes all unsewered industrial shanty towns smell alike. What I have gotten used to was, however, but a whiff from the dense atmosphere of Paris under Louis XIV and Louis XV. Only during the last year of his reign was an ordinance passed which made the removal of fecal matter from the corridors of the palace of Versailles a weekly procedure. Below the windows of the Ministry of Finance pigs were slaughtered for decades and the wall of the palace was impregnated with layers of blood. Even tanneries still worked in the city — albeit on the shores of the Seine. People relieved themselves as a matter of course against the wall of any dwelling or church. The odor of shallow graves was part of the deads' presence within the walls. So much was this atmosphere taken for granted that the surviving sources barely call attention to it.

This olfactory nonchalance came to an end when a small number of citizens lost their tolerance towards the stench from burial places within churches. Without any indication that the physical procedures by which corpses were entombed near the altar had changed since the Middle Ages, in 1737 the Parliament of Paris appointed a commission to study the danger they represented to public health. The miasma emanating from graves was declared dangerous to the living. Within the decade a treatise by the Abbé Charles-Gabriel Porée, Fenelon's librarian, was edited several times. In this book, the theologian argued that philosophical and juridical considerations demanded that the dead be laid to rest outside the city. According to Philippe Ariès, the new olfactory sensitivity to the presence of corpses was due to a new kind of fear of death. During the third quarter of the century, reports that people had died from mere stench became commonplace. From Scotland to Poland people do not just resent but fear the stench of decomposing bodies. Mass deaths among the members of church congregations occurring within the hour after exposure to the miasma escaping from a grave opened for a funeral, are described by supposed witnesses. While in the 1760s the Cimetière des Innocents is much used for parties in the afternoon and for illicit intercourse during the night, it was closed by general request of the people by 1780, because of the intolerable smell of decomposing bodies.

Intolerance against the smell of feces took much longer to develop, although the first complaints about its intensity can be heard in the 1740s. Attention was drawn to the issue at first only by public-spirited scientists who studied 'the airs' — today we would say gases. The instruments for the study of volatile substances were still rudimentary at the time; the existence of oxygen and its place in combustion had not yet been understood. Researchers had to rely on their noses for the analysis they made. But this did not stop them from publishing treatises on the subject of the cities' 'exhalations.' A dozen and a half such essays and books published between mid-century and Napoleon are known. These treatises deal with the seven smelly points of the human body that lie between the top of the head and the interstices between the toes; they classify the seven odors of decomposition that can be observed in succession in a rotting animal body; they distinguish disagreeable odors into those which are healthy, like dung and shit, and those which are putrid and damaging; they teach how to bottle smells for later comparison and the study of their evolution; they estimate the weight per capita exudations of city dwellers and the effect of their deposit — by air — in the city's vicinity. Most of the new concern with malodorous miasma is given expression by a small group of physicians, philosophers, and publicists. In almost every instance the authors complain about the insensitivity of the public at large toward the need to remove these 'bad airs' from the city.

By the end of the century this avant-garde of deodorizers begins to count on the support of a small but important minority within the city. On several accounts, social attitudes towards bodily waste began to change. The king's audience on the stool (*en selle*) had been abandoned two generations ago. By mid-century we have the first report that at a large ball, separate closets for women were provided. Finally, Marie Antoinette had a door installed to privatize her defecation, making it into an intimate function.

First the procedure, then also the outcome were pushed beyond the reach of eye and nose. Underwear that could be frequently washed, as well as the bidet, came into fashion. To sleep between sheets and in one's separate bed was now charged with moral and medical significance. Soon heavy blankets came to be proscribed, because they accumulate body-aura and lead to wet dreams. Medical men discovered that a sick man's odor could infect the healthy, and the single hospital bed became a hygienic exigency if not a praxis. Then on November 15th, 1793, the Revolutionary Convention solemnly declared each man's right to his own bed as part of the rights of man. A private buffer of space surrounding each one in bed, on the stool, and in the grave became an exigency of the citizen's dignity. Charities were formed to spare the poor at least one of the new horrors: burial in a mass grave.

Hand in hand with the new toilet training of the bourgeoisie, the social toilet of the city itself became the predominant urban problem. Since the early eighteenth century the particularly unhealthy conditions of prisons and bedlams had attracted international attention. The wide attention given to their knee-deep filth had even helped to make the rest of the city look clean by comparison. Now the high mortality rates in the prison were related to the intensity of their smell perceptible over a distance. The ventilator was invented and the first ones installed to give a whiff of fresh air, at least to those spaces where the innocent prisoners were kept. The 'airing' of prisoners seemed to be necessary, but difficult to organize. So several cities from Switzerland to Belgium adopted the idea of the city of Berne to combine removal of excrements with the ventilation of prisoners by using a new machine. This was a cart drawn by chained men, to which women were attached on thinner chains, that allowed them to move with relative freedom over the pavement to collect waste, dead animals and nightsoil. The city came to be compared with the organism, it too having its smelly points. Smell began to become class specific. The poor are those who smell, and often do not know it. Osmology — the study of smells — tried to establish itself as a separate science. Supposed experiments proved that savages smell differently from Europeans. Samojeds, Negroes and Hottentots can be each recognized by their racial smell, which is independent from the diet they eat or from how much they wash.

To be well-bred came to mean to be clean: not to smell and have no odor attached to one's aura and home. By the beginning of the nineteenth century women were bred to cultivate their own, individual fragrance. This ideal had appeared during the end of the *Ancien Régime*, at the time when the strong and traditional animal perfumes like ambergris, musk and civet were abandoned in favor of toilet waters and plant oils. Napoleon's upstart preference for the old tradition led to a short-lived return to the use of precious animal fat from rodents' genitals; but by the time of Napoleon III their use had become a sign of debauchery. The well-to-do lady now enhanced her personal flair with vegetal fragrances which are much more volatile, must be reapplied frequently, stay lingering in the domestic sphere and become signs of conspicuous consumption. Rousseau's Emile now learns that 'fragrance does not give as much as it makes you hope for.' The separate, mirror-walled cabinets, one for the faucet and one for the sink, which an opera-singer, Mlle Deschamps, had brought from England to the embarrassment of Frenchmen in 1750, were part of exalted propriety two generations later. As the rich are lightly scented with vegetable oils, and the not-so-rich are increasingly well-scrubbed and taught to leave their shoes outside the door, the deodorizing of the poor majority became a major goal of the medical police.

During the first half of the nineteenth century, the English have already set out to wash their cities and to pollute the Thames. In France and in general on the Continent, public opinion is not yet ready for such profligacy. L'Institut, in a report of 1835, rejects the proposal to channel the excrements of Paris into the Seine. It is not concern for the river, nor mere anti-English prejudice, which motivated this decision, but the calculation of the enormous economic value that would thus be lost. Another twenty years later the editors of the Journal of Medical Chemistry invoke Malthus and arguments from social physiology to demonstrate that canalizing excrements is a public misdeed. During the years preceding their study the proposal had been heard to tie the distribution of old age pensions to the old citizen's daily delivery of select fertilizers that they had collected. Now that the railroad had come to the city, it ought to be used to allow the city to fertilize the countryside, possibly turning it into a garden.

By the 1860s two national ideologies on the value of sewers faced each other across the channel. Victor Hugo gave the supreme literary expression to the French position. 'La merde,' since Cambronne's exclamation, must be considered as something very French and of great commercial potential. In *Les Misérables* it feeds '*l'intestin du Léviathan.*' No doubt, he says, the sewer of Paris for the last ten centuries has been the city's disease but '*L'égout est le vice que la ville a dans le sang.*' Any attempt to stuff more night soil down the drain could not but increase the already unimaginable horrors of the city's cloaca. To live in the city calls for us to accept its smell.

The opposite view on the value of sewers and the disvalue of shit was taken in 1871 by the Prince of Wales, before he became King Edward VII. If he were not the prince, he said, his next preference would be that of becoming a plumber. In the Royal Society of the Arts, Hellinger about that time exhorted his fellows: 'Lying there in these strong arms of yours, slumbering peacefully in their hardened muscles, resting in the well-trained fingers and educated hands is the health of this Leviathan city'! Jules Verne in a novel gives the French literary expression to this English view: 'to clean, forever to clean, destroying the miasma as soon as it rises from human agglomeration, that is the principal and foremost task of central governments.' The sweat of the laboring classes was dangerous as long as it smelled.

To deodorize the city the English architects proposed to use water. As early as 1596 Sir John Harrington, the godson of Queen Elizabeth I, had invented the water closet and published a treatise on 'Ajax,' but the contraption remained for most people a curiosity. Then, in 1851 George Jennings installed public W.C.'s in the Crystal Palace for the Great Exhibition and 827,280 persons, 14% of the visitors, tried them and paid for their use. The 'convenience suited to the advanced age of civilization' was perfected by a Mr Crapper, a foundry owner. The '*anus mirabilis*' water flush reserve valve was patented in England, and the English word 'W.C.' became an integral part of every civilized language. According to a U.S. Government report, Baltimore was the last Eastern city to produce its fertilizer 'in a natural way' before it switched to mandatory flush in 1912.

By the end of the nineteenth century fecal-borne infections began to seep into tap water. Engineers were faced with the choice to apply limited economic and institutional resources either to the treatment of sewage before its disposal or the treatment of the water supply. For the first half of this century, the accent was placed on the sterilization of the supply. Only recently had bacteriology replaced the old filth theory that explained illness as the result of corruption within the body, by the new germ-theory of disease which constantly threatens the body with microbe-invasions. Citizens demanded above all to be supplied with 'germless drinking water' from their taps. Then, towards mid-century, what came from the tap had ceased to be odorless and had become a liquid many people no longer dared to drink. The transformation of H_2O into a cleaning fluid was complete. Public emphasis could shift toward the 'purification' of sewage and the salvaging of lakes. In the United States the cost of sewage treatment and collection by 1980 has become the greatest expense of local government. Only schools cost more.

For the archaic Greeks, I guess, ritual lustrations exorcized miasma more often than not. The attempt to wash the city of its evil smells has obviously failed. At the plush club in Dallas, where I slept, little bottles with cotton tongues spread a powerful anesthetic that paralyzes the nasal mucus to mask the failure of the most costly plumbing that you can buy. The deodorant cripples perception with pink noise for the nose. Our cities have become places of historically unprecedented industrial stench. And we have become as insensitive to this pollution as the citizens of the early eighteenth century of Paris were toward their corpses and their excrements.

We have now followed the waters of history from archaic Greece to the ecological tap. We have looked at the fountains of Rome that flushed titanic Mnemosyne from the mind of the literate city and peopled it with classical nymphs. And we have looked at the waterworks that remove H_2O out of sight. We have listened to the improvisations of gurgling springs, to the planned symphony of the fountain of Trevi, and then to the hiss of faucets, the dripping of sinks and the sound of flush. We have understood that city water, in Western culture, has a beginning and, therefore, might have an end. It is born when the artist domesticated each of the waters of Rome at an appropriate fountain where it was used to tell its own unique story to the citizens' dreams, and it is threatened when the suction rotors of waterworks make it into a cleaner and coolant of which some may be diverted into a lake. We have come to wonder about the possibility of coexistence between wealth and dreams.

Looking back at the waters that have flowed through the cities, we can now recognize their importance for dreams. Only where dreams have been reflected on the waters of the commons, cities could be spun out of their stuff. Only waters alive with nymphs and with memories can fuse the archetypal and the historical side of dreams. H_2O is not water in this sense. H_2O is a liquid that has been stripped of both its cosmic meaning and of its *genius loci*. It is opaque to dreams. City water has debauched the *commons* of dreams.

A Plea for Research on Lay Literacy

Special Guest Lecture at the American
Education Research Association General Assembly
San Francisco, August 1986

By lay literacy I mean a symbolic fallout from the use of the
alphabet in Western cultures — something quite different
from clerical literacy, which consists in the ability to read
and write. By lay literacy I mean a distinct mode of
perception in which the book becomes the decisive metaphor
through which we conceive of the Self and its place. By lay
literacy I do not mean the spread of written contents beyond
the pale of the clerics to others who, previously, could only
listen to what is being read to them. I use the term lay
literacy to speak of a mind-frame which is defined by a set of
certainties which spread within the realm of the alphabet
since late medieval times. The lay-literate is certain that
speech can be frozen, that memories can be stored and
retrieved, that secrets can be engraved in conscience and
therefore examined, that experience can be described. By lay
literacy I mean therefore a weaving together of categories
that — since the twelfth century — has shaped the mental
space of the 'illiterate' laity just as much as that of the
'literate' clergy. It constitutes a new type of space inside
which social reality is reconstructed: a new kind of network
of fundamental assumptions about all that can be seen or
known. I have tried to follow the evolution of this mind-set
since the Middle Ages, along with the transformation of a
number of certainties that can exist only within it. I will
illustrate how such a transformation happens by telling the
story of 'the text.'

The literate mind of the non-reader

Two reasons commend the history of lay literacy to the attention of people who pursue research on, and not only in, education. The first is the new level of concern within the educational enterprise with universal clerical literacy as a goal to be reached before the year 2000. The other is the powerful temptation to replace the book as the fundamental metaphor of self-perception by the metaphor of the computer.

As to the first, we are all aware that new psychological, managerial and electronic techniques are being used to spread, in one more attempt, the clerical skills of reading and writing. Whether, and if so how, these literacy campaigns interact with lay literacy ought to be better understood. Fifty years ago Luria studied the major shifts that occur in mental activity as people acquire clerical literacy. Their cognitive processes cease to be mainly concrete and situational. They begin to draw inferences, not only on the basis of their own practical experience, but on assumptions formulated in language. Since 1931, when Luria did these studies in Stalinist Russia, much has been learned about the change which clerical literacy induces in perception, representation, reasoning, imagination and self-awareness. But in most of the studies, a causal link is assumed to exist between the individual's writing skill and the new mind-frame he acquires. As I will show, in the light of the history of lay literacy, this assumption is largely false. Since the Middle Ages, the certainties that characterize the literate mind have spread, overwhelmingly, by means other than instruction in the skills of reading and writing. This is a point which must be kept in mind in the current discussions on illiteracy, semi-literacy and post-literacy. The approach currently used in spreading the skill of 'written communication' might actually be subversive to the literate mind.

While I want to call your attention to this independence of the literate mind from personal writing skills, my main argument centers on the current transmogrification of the literate mind itself. During the last decade, the computer has rapidly been replacing the book as the prime metaphor to visualize the Self, its activities and its relatedness to the environment. Words have been reduced to 'message units,' speech to the 'use of language,' conversation to something called 'oral communication,' and the text has been reduced from a string of sound symbols to one of 'bytes.' I want to argue that the mental space into which literacy certainties fit, and that *other* mental space engendered by certainties about the Turing Machine, are heteronomous spaces. The study of the mental space that is generated by lay literacy seems to me a necessary step if we are to grasp the nature of that entirely different mental space which is becoming dominant in our time. And just as lay literacy is largely independent of the individual's clerical skills, so the cybernetic mind is largely independent of the individual's technical proficiency with a computer.

Solid foundations for research on the literate mind have been laid; I only plead that the results of this research be applied in education, to recognize unacknowledged postulates which are implied in the axioms from which educational theories are derived. The first to observe the depth of the epistemological break between oral and literate existence was Millman Parry, some sixty years ago. Through him we come to recognize the Island of Literacy that rises out of the magma of epic orality as a potter-scribe takes down the song of a bard, which we call the Illiad. His pupil, Albert Lord, convinces us that the steps by which one becomes a bard cannot be grasped with the same concepts as those used to get at the steps by which one becomes a literate poet. Eric Havelock argues convincingly that the profound changes in the style of reasoning, in the mode of perceiving the universe, in the appearance of 'literature' and science in sixth- and fifth-century B.C., Greece can be understood only in light of a transition from an oral to a literate mind. Others have explored how the unique and once- and-for-all invention of the alphabet spread to Brahmin India and thence to the Orient. The circumstances under which new European people were brought into the realm of literate perception are well known to me and, therefore, I take my main examples from that epoch. Elisabeth Eisenstein, in her monumental study on the impact of the printing press on Renaissance culture, deals with another major transformation within the literate mind in yet another epoch. Jack Goody, the anthropologist, has turned our attention to the ever- ongoing 'alphabetization of the savage mind.' And Walter Ong, over the last two decades, has pulled together the research of psychologists, anthropologists and students of epics, to argue that alphabetization is equivalent to the 'technologization' of the word. So far, however, no one has attempted a history of the literate mind as distinct from clerical literacy. And it is a daunting task. The literate mind is a phenomenon both brilliantly clear and slippery — like a jellyfish whose features and shapes can be discerned only so long as it is observed within its own milieu.

The irrelevance of schooling to the literate mind

To make my plea for this novel research plausible, I will explain the steps which led me to my present position. This I can do by criticizing my book, *Deschooling Society*, for its naive views. My travelogue begins twenty years ago when that book was about to appear. During the nine months the manuscript was at the publishers, I grew more and more dissatisfied with its text which, by the way, did not argue for the elimination of schools. This misapprehension I owe to Cass Canfield Sr, Harper's president, who named my baby and, in doing so, misrepresented my thoughts. The book advocates the *disestablishment* of schools, in the sense in which the Church has been disestablished in the United States. I called for the 'disestablishment of schools' for the sake of education and here, I noticed, lay my mistake. Much more important than the disestablishment of schools — I now see — was the reversal of those trends which make of education a pressing need rather than a gift of gratuitous leisure. I began to fear that the disestablishment of the educational church would lead to a fanatic revival of many forms of degraded education.

Norman Cousins published my own recantation in the *Saturday Review* during the very week my book came out. In it I argued that the alternative to schooling was not some other type of educational agency, or the design of educational opportunities in every aspect of life, but a society which fosters a different attitude of people toward tools. Since then, my curiosity and reflections have focused on the historical circumstances under which the very idea of educational needs can arise.

So that you might see the character of my argument, let me tell you how I came to the study of education. I came from theology. As a theologian, I specialized in ecclesiology, which constitutes the only old learned tradition which — in social analysis — distinguishes fundamentally between two entities: the visible community in which the spirit is embodied, and the quite different community which is the city or the state. This dualism is of its essence. Emboldened by 1500 years of ecclesiology, I saw the Church as more than a mere metaphor for the new Alma Mater. I tended increasingly to stress the fundamental continuity between two seemingly opposed agencies, at least insofar as they defined the meaning of education in successive centuries.

Within ecclesiology, the study of Liturgy has always been my favorite topic. This branch of learning deals with the role of cult in bringing about the phenomenon, Church. Liturgy studies how solemn gestures and chants, hierarchies and ritual objects create not only faith, but the reality of the community-as-Church, which is the object of this faith. Comparative liturgy sharpens the eye to distinguish the essential mythopoetic (myth-making) rituals from accidents of style. So sensitized, I began to look on those things that go on within schools as parts of a liturgy. Accustomed to the great beauty of Christian Liturgy, I was of course put off by the abject style so proper to schools.

I then began to study the place that the liturgy of schooling holds in the social construction of modern reality, and the degree to which it creates the need for education. I began to discern the traces which schooling leaves on the mind-set of its participants. I focused my attention on the effects of scholastic liturgy by putting into parenthesis not only learning theory, but also research which measures the achievement of learning goals. In the articles published in *Deschooling Society*, I presented a phenomenology of schooling. From Brooklyn to Bolivia it consists of age-specific assemblies around a so-called teacher, for three to six hours on 200 days of the year; yearly promotions which also celebrate the exclusion of those who fail or who are banished into a lower stratum; subject matter more detailed and carefully chosen than any known monastic Liturgy.

Everywhere attendence varies from 12 to 48 pupils, and teachers are those who have absorbed several years of this mumbo-jumbo in excess of their pupils. Everywhere, pupils are judged to have acquired some 'education' — which school by definition monopolizes — and which is thought necessary to make pupils into valuable citizens, each knowing at which class level he has dropped out of this 'preparation for life.' I then saw how the liturgy of schooling creates the social reality in which education is perceived as a necessary good. And I was even then aware how enveloping, lifelong education could, in the last two decades of the twentieth century, replace schooling in its myth-making function. However, I did not suspect what I now propose as a subject for research: the waning of the traditional key concepts of *literate* education, since the terms for them are used in analogy with computer program language. I did not then conceive of schooling as one of the masks behind which this transmogrification could take place.

At the time I was engaged in these reflections we were at the height of the international development effort. One could see that school was like a world-wide stage on which the hidden assumptions of economic progress were being acted out. The school system demonstrated where development could not but lead: to international, standardized stratification; to universal dependence on service; to counter-productive specialization; to the degradation of the many for the sake of a few. As I wrote *Deschooling*, the social effects, and not the historical substance of education, were still at the core of my interest. I still accepted that, fundamentally, educational needs of some kind were a historical given of human nature.

Constitution and evolution of a mental sphere

My acceptance of the unexamined assumption that by nature human beings belong to the species of *homo educandus* started to dim as I studied the history of economic concepts from Mandeville to Marx (with Réné Dumont), and from Bentham to Walrass (with Elie Halévy) and, as I became aware of the historical nature of my own certainties regarding scarcity through reading Karl Polanyi. I recognized that in economics there exists an important critical tradition which analyzes as historical constructs the assumptions which economists of all colors make. I became aware that *homo œconomicus*, with whom we identify emotionally and intellectually, is of quite recent creation. And thus I came to understand education as 'learning,' *when it takes place under the assumption of scarcity in the means which produce it.* The 'need' for education in this perspective appears as the result of societal beliefs and arrangements which make the means for so-called socialization scarce. And, in this same perspective, I began to notice that educational rituals reflected, rein- forced and actually created belief in the value of learning pursued under conditions of scarcity. With rather limited success, I have tried to encourage my students to do for the field of pedagogics what others have done in the field of economics.

Polanyi shows that the exchange of goods predates by many centuries, if not millenia, the economic marketing of commodities. This pre-economic exchange is performed by status traders who act more like diplomats than business- men. Commenting on the *Politics* of Aristotle, Polanyi shows that the technique of marketing, in which the value of a good is made to depend on demand and supply and provides a profit for the merchant, is a Greek invention of the early fourth century B.C. I then found increasing evidence that the conceptual space within which *paideia* acquired a meaning comparable to what we call education, was defined at about the same time. What Polanyi calls the 'dis-embedding' of a formal economic sphere within society happens during the same decade in which a formal educational sphere is also dis-embedded.

During the same century Euclidian space came into formal existence. Its creation and destiny provide a useful analogy to illustrate what I mean by 'a mental space.' Euclid was careful to state the axioms on which he built his geometry. He wanted them remembered as stipulations. However, as we moderns are now acutely aware, in one instance he stated as a self-evident axiom something which in fact requires a postulate. When Euclid stated as axiomatic that two parallel lines never intersect, he unknowingly implied the existence of only one space, namely, the particular one now named after him. He made an assumption which, remaining unexamined, turned into a certainty. And, for 2000 years, Western learned tradition took it as a natural fact. Not until the turn of our century did Riemann demonstrate that a space in which two parallel lines never intersect is, for the mathematician, only a special case.

Soon after Riemann laid the mathematical foundation for relativity, anthropologists noticed that the members of many cultures do not see with Euclidian eyes. Ethnolinguists then confirmed that, for instance, Hopis or Dogons speak about space and directions in ways that can more easily be translated into the terms of mathematical tensors than into any Indo-Germanic language. On the other hand, historians found that ancient literatures describe space much more thoroughly by reference to smells, sounds and the experience of moving through an atmosphere than by evoking visual experience. Art historians like Panofsky and philosophers like Susan Langer, have made plausible that most artists paint the space which they and their epoch see. They do not organize their perception in the perspective that Dürer created, or within the coordinates of Descartes. Perspective, so the argument goes, was introduced into painting to express the newly-found ability to see the world predominantly in a self-centered way. Parallel to Kuhn's chain of descriptive paradigms succeeding each other in the sciences, art historians find successive descriptive paradigms which correspond to distinct ways of perceiving visual space.

Revolution by the alphabet

No attempt comparable with the historiography of economic or visual space has so far been made to explore the constitution and evolution of the mental space within which pedagogical ideas take their shape. This does not mean that all academic disciplines have remained prisoners of one space; it only means that the principal challenge to this mental confinement has come from non-educators and, so far, has not been acknowledged within the educational profession. Millman Parry's discovery of the heteronomy between oral and alphabetic existence could have made educators recognize the questionable postulates which they unknowingly accept as the axioms of their field. But the relevance of Parry's discovery for a historical theory of education has so far gone unnoticed.

In his doctoral thesis on Homeric epithets (1926), Parry was the first to notice that the transition from epic orality to written poetry in archaic Greece marks an epistemic break. He argued that for the literate mind it is nearly impossible to imagine the context within which the pre-literate bard composes his songs. No bridge built out of the certainties inherent in the literate mind can lead back into the oral magma. I cannot here sum up the insights and conclusions reached during the last fifty years by Lord, Havelock, Peabody, Notopoulos and Ong — the work which convinced me. But, for those who have not followed their writings on the heteronomy of epic orality and literate poetry, let me briefly note some of the firm conclusions I draw. In an oral culture there can be no 'word' such as we are accustomed to look up in the dictionary. In that kind of culture, what silence brackets may be a syllable or a sentence, but not our atom, the word. Further, all utterances are winged, forever gone before they are fully pronounced. The idea of fixing these sounds into a line, of mummifying them for later resurrection, cannot occur. Therefore memory, in an oral culture, cannot be conceived as a storage room or a wax tablet. Urged on by the lyre, the bard does not 'look up' the right word; rather, a fitting utterance from the grab-bag of traditional phrases moves his tongue to the appropriate beat. Homer, the bard, never tried and rejected *le mot juste*. But Virgil changed and corrected the *Aeneid* up to the hour of his death; he was already the prototype of the literate poet, the genial *Schrift-Steller*.

Appropriately, the equivalent of our curriculum was called *Musiké* in the schools of fifth-century Athens. Students learned to compose music; writing remained a servile skill exercised mostly by potters until around the year 400 B.C., when Plato went to school. Only then does true subject matter come into being; only then can the wisdom of a previous generation be transmitted in that generation's words, to be commented upon in distinct and new words by the teacher. Alphabetic recording is as much a condition for what we call science/literature, as it is necessary for the distinction between thought and speech. Plato, one of the few giants who struggles with the divide between orality and literacy, makes this transition from ever newly recalled experience to literate memory the subject of his *Phaedrus*. He was acutely aware that with the teacher who sows (written) words, which can neither speak for themselves nor teach the truth adequately to others (*Phaedr.* 276a), an entirely new epoch was opening, and that the use of the alphabet would bar a return to the oral past.

With more clarity than the moderns, Plato seems to have been aware that with literacy a new mental space had come into existence and, within it, previously unimagined concepts that would give an entirely new meaning to the upbringing of Lysias. Two things therefore can be distinguished in the history of educational assumptions: the beginning of pedagogical space — which might now be threatened — and the transformations of the web of pedagogical concepts that take place within this space.

To demonstrate how one such axiom fitting literate space

has expanded and acquired a certain dominance, I offer as example 'the text.' The word is classical: in Latin *textus* is a woven fabric and — only rarely — the composition of well-running words. At the time of the Lindisfarne Bible, the word is first used as an equivalent for Holy Scripture. Then, in the fourteenth century, it is actually used for the concept which we now take for granted, a concept which — as I will immediately show — under different designations had already appeared 200 years earlier. I want to speak about the emergence of the idea or concept, not about the use of the term.

Revolution by the text

I choose the idea of the text for two reasons: the idea is important in educational theory, and — thoroughly transmogrified — it is also central to communication theory. From the mid-twelfth century onward, the text is past speech, so encoded that the eye can pick it up from the page; in communication theory, the term stands for any binary sequence. The text, as a hinge element within the literate mind, has a beginning and an end.

By definition, the alphabet is a technique to record speech sounds in visible form. In this sense it is much more than any other notational system. The reader who is faced by ideograms, hieroglyphs, or even the non-vocalized Semitic beta-bet, must understand the sense of the line before he can pronounce it. Only the alphabet makes it possible to read correctly without any understanding. And, in fact, for well over 2000 years, the decoding of the alphabetic record could not be performed by the eye alone. 'Reading' meant loud or mumbled recitation. Augustine, the champion orator of his time, was surprised when he discovered that it was possible to engage in silent reading. In the *Confessions* he tells of his discovery: he learned to read without making a noise and without waking his brethren.

While occasionally practiced, silent reading would have been normally impossible until the seventh century; the break or empty space between words was unknown. Only a few monumental inscriptions spoke to the eye by separating word from word. On wax tablets, papyrus or parchment, each line was an uninterrupted sequence of letters. There was almost no other way of reading than rehearsing the sentences aloud and listening to hear whether they made sense. Mere *dicta* — speech fragments out of context — were practically unreadable. A sentence, meant for the record, was 'dictated'; it was spoken in *cursus*, the classical prose-rhythm which we have now lost. By getting the hang of the *cursus* that the *dictator* had chosen, reading by sight became possible. The sense remained buried on the page until it had been voiced.

Word breaks were introduced in Bede's time (672–735) as a didactic device. They were meant to facilitate the acquisition of Latin vocabulary by 'thickheaded Scottish novices.' As a side effect, the procedure of copying manuscripts changed. Thus far, either the original had to be dictated by one monk to several scribes, or each scribe had to read aloud as many words as he could keep in his auditory memory, and then write them down while 'dictating to himself.' Spaces between words made silent copying possible; the copyist could now transcribe word for word. The earlier line, made up of an uninterrupted sequence of thirty to fifty minuscules, just could not have been copied at sight.

Even though the codex of the Middle Ages then contained visibly separated words rather than the unbroken Indian line of letters, it still did not make the text visible. This new reality takes shape only after the death of Bernard and Abelard. It is brought forth by the convergence of two dozen techniques, some with Arabic, others with Classical antecedents, some entirely new. These innovations together conspire to support and shape a substantially new idea: that of a text which is distinct both from the book and from its readings.

Chapters get titles, and these are divided by sub-titles. Chapter and verse are now numbered; quotations are marked by underlining with a different color ink; paragraphs are introduced and, occasionally, marginal glosses summarize their subject; miniatures become less ornamental and more illustrative. Thanks to these new devices, a table of contents and an alphabetical subject index now could be prepared, and references from one part to the other could be made within chapters. The book that formerly could only be read through is now made accessible at random: the idea of consultation acquires a new meaning. Books can now be chosen and picked up in a new mode. At the beginning of the twelfth century, it was still the custom that on certain feast days of each season, the abbot would solemnly take the books from the treasury where they were kept with jewels and relics of saints, and lay them out in the chapter room. Each monk then picked one for his *lectio* during the following months. By the end of this same century, books were moved out of the ark in the sacristy and begin to be stored in a separate library, well titled, on shelves. The first catalogs are made of the monastery's holdings, and by the end of the next century Paris and Oxford each boast of a union catalog.

Thanks to these technical changes, consultation, the checking of quotations and silent reading become common, and *scriptoria* ceased to be places where each one tried to hear his own voice. Neither the teacher nor the neighbor can now hear what is being read and, partly as a result, both bawdy and heretical books multiply. As the old habit of quoting from a well-trained memory palace was replaced by the new skill of citing right out of the book, the idea of a text which is independent from this or that manuscript becomes visible. Many of the social effects which have often been attributed to the printing press were in fact already the result of a text that can be looked up. The old clerical skill of taking dictation and reading out lines is now complemented by the skills of contemplating and searching the text with the eyes. And, in a complex way, the new reality of the text and the new clerical skill affect the literate mind, common to clerisy and laity alike.

For most practical purposes, penmanship and clerical status coincided until well into the fourteenth century. The mere ability to sign and spell was taken as proof of clerical privilege, and anyone who could demonstrate such capacity escaped capital punishment — he enjoyed clerical privilege.

But while the majority of clerics were still much too unskilled to 'look up' the text of a book, 'the text' became a constitutive metaphor for a vast lay population's entire mode of existence during the fifteenth century.

For those who are not medievalists but still desire a solid introduction to what is known to historians about the growing lay literacy of the West at that time, I recommend a book by Martin Clanchy, *From Memory to Written Record*. He stresses not what clerical literacy contributed to literature and science, but how the spread of letters changed the self-perception of the age and ideas about society. In England, for instance, the number of charters used in the transfer of properties increased by a factor of one hundred or more between the early twelfth and the late thirteenth century. Further, the written charter replaced the oath, which is oral by its very nature. The 'testament' replaced the clod of soil which the father had formerly put into the hand of the son whom he had chosen as heir to his lands. In court, a writ got the last word! Possession, an activity exercised by *sitting upon*, *sedere*, was overshadowed in importance by the 'holding' (tenancy, maintenance) of a title, something one does with the hand. Formerly, you solemnly walked with the buyer around the property that you wanted to sell; now you learned to point it out with your finger, and had the notary describe it. Even the illiterate acquired the certainty that the world is owned by description: 'thirty steps from the rock shaped like a dog, and then to the brook in a straight line. . .' Everyone now tended to become a *dictator*, even though scribes remained few. Surprisingly, even serfs carried seals, to put beneath their *dictation*.

Everyone now keeps records, even the devil. Under the new guise of a hellish scribe, portrayed as the 'writing devil,' he appears in late Romanesque sculpture. He squats on his coiled tail and prepares the record of every deed, word and thought of his clients for the final reckoning. Simultaneously, a representation of the Final Judgment appears in the tympanum above the main entrance of the parish church. It represents Christ, enthroned as a judge between the gates of heaven and the jaws of hell, with an angel holding the Book of Life opened at the page corresponding to the individual Poor Soul. Even the rudest peasant and humblest char-woman can no longer enter the church portal without learning that their name and deeds appear in the text of the heavenly Book. God, like the landlord, refers to the written account of a past which, in the community, has been mercifully forgotten. In 1215, the Fourth Lateran Council makes auricular confession obligatory. The Counciliar text is the first canonical document which explicitly states that an obligation is binding on all Christians, *both* men and women. And confession interiorizes the sense of the text in two distinct ways: it fosters the sense of 'memory' and of 'confession.' For a millennium, Christians had recited their prayers as they picked them up within the community, with great local and generational variants. Sentences were often so corrupted that they might foster piety, but certainly did not make sense. The twelfth-century Church Synods tried to remedy this state of affairs. Their canons imposed on the clergy the duty of training the laity's memory by having them repeat the words of the *Pater* and *Credo* word for word as they are in the Book. When the penitent went to confession, he had to prove to the priest that he knew his prayers by heart, that he had acquired the kind of memory on which words could be engraved. Only after this memory test could he proceed to the examination of another spot of his heart, henceforth called his conscience, in which the account of his evil deeds, words and thoughts had been kept. Even the illiterate 'I' that speaks in confession now perceives through new, literate eyes its own 'Self' in the image of a text.

Lay self, lay conscience, lay memory

The new kind of past, frozen in letters, is cemented as much in the self as in society, in memory and conscience as much as in charters and account books, in descriptions and signed confessions. And the experience of an individual self corre-sponds to a new kind of subject of the law which takes shape in the law schools of Bologna and Paris, and becomes normative, over the centuries, for the conception of *person*, wherever Western society extends its influence. This new self and this new society are realities which can arise only within the literate mind.

In an oral society a past statement can only be recalled by a similar one. Even in societies where non-alphabetic notations are kept, speech does not lose its wings; once uttered, it is gone forever. Pictographic or ideographic notation suggests to the reader an idea for which he must, anew, find a word. The alphabetic text fixes the sound. When it is read, the past *dictator's* sentences become present. A new kind of building material for the present has come into being; it is made up of the actual words of speakers long dead. And, in the late Middle Ages, the constitution of the visible text brings whole constructions from the past, in a new way, into the present.

In an oral society, a man has to stand by his word. He confirms his word by taking an oath, which is a conditional curse called upon himself in the event that he should become unfaithful. While swearing he grasps at his beard or his balls, pledging his flesh as a troth. When a freeman swears, any case against him comes to rest. But under a literate regime, the oath pales before the manuscript; it is no longer recall, but the record that counts. And if there is no record, the judge is empowered to read the heart of the accused. So torture is introduced into the proceedings. The question is applied and pries open the heart. Confession under torture now takes the place of oath and ordeal. Inquisitorial techniques teach the accused to accept the identity between the text that the court reads out to him and that other text which is etched in his heart. Only in the visual comparison of two texts can the identity of the two contents — that of the original and that of the copy — be imagined. A miniature of 1226 preserves the first picture of the 'corrector,' a new official who leans over the shoulder of the scribe to certify the 'identity' between two charters. It is again a clerical technique which is reflected in the new law of judicial evidence which demands that the judge check the defendant's utterance against the truth at the bottom of his heart.

The literate mind implies a profound reconstruction of the lay self, the lay conscience, the lay memory, no less than the lay conception of the past and the lay fear of having to face the Doomsday Book at the hour of death. All of these new features, of course, the laity and the clergy share: and they are effectively transmitted outside of schools and scriptoria. So far, this point has been largely neglected by historians of education. They have mainly focused on the evolution of clerical literacy and have seen in these transformations of mental space but a side-product of chancellery skills. Historians have well explored the style of letters, of abbreviation, of integration between text and ornament. They have enlarged our knowledge of the impact that paper-making and the new smooth writing surface had on the evolution of a cursive script in the thirteenth century, something which enabled scholastic masters to lecture from notes written by their own hand rather than dictated. They have observed the enormous increase in sealing wax used in chancelleries. They can tell us that, for a typical court session in the mid-twelfth century, barely a dozen sheep would lose their skin, while a century later several hundred hides would be needed to make the necessary parchment.

If historians have paid attention to the evolution of lay literacy, or more generally to the new configuration taken by the literate mind, they have usually observed how it takes shape among clerics, how the new self came to be explored as a new psychological domain in the autobiographies of someone like Guibert and Abelard, how new scholastic logic and grammar presupposed the visual textualization of the page. At best, some historians have attempted to understand how the increasing frequency with which *fabliaux* romances, travelogues and homilies were written for reading in front of a large public had affected the style in which these were composed. Yet, obviously, while schools and scriptoria and the new technical notions of clerical literacy were essential to the spread of the literate mind among clerics, these were not the means through which lay literacy spread.

The details I have given, taken from the later twelfth century which I know best, all illustrate what I mean by the impact which one particular literate technique can have on the shape of an epoch's literate mind. They illustrate the effect which the visible text had at that moment on a web of other concepts which, in their formation, are dependent on the alphabet. I point to such notions as self, conscience, memory, possessive description, identity. It would be the historian's task to establish the epochs of this web, its transformation under the influence of late medieval *narratio*, of 'fiction,' of Renaissance critical text editions, of the printing press, of vernacular grammar, of the 'reader.' At each stage, the historian of education would get new inspiration by starting his inquiry from the evidence of new forms of lay literacy rather than from new ideals and techniques of teachers. However, my plea for research is not primarily motivated by my interest in this neglected side of educational research, dealing with phenomena that take place within the alphabetic culture space. My main reason for pleading for this research is concerned with the exploration of that space itself. I feel my very self threatened by the waning of this space.

Exile of the literate mind

I still remember a shock I had in Chicago in 1964. We were sitting around a seminar table; opposite me sat a young anthropologist. At the critical point of what I thought was a conversation, he said to me, 'Illich, you can't turn me on, you do not communicate with me.' For the first time in my life I became aware that I was being addressed not as a person but as a transmitter. After a moment of disarray, I began to feel outrage. A live person, to whom I thought that I had been responding, experienced our dialogue as something more general, namely as 'one form of human communication.' I immediately thought of Freud's description of three instances of sickening outrage which were experienced in Western culture: the *Kränkungen* when the heliocentric system, the theory of evolution, and the postulate of the unconscious had to be integrated into everyday thinking. It is then, twenty-five years ago, that I began to reflect on the depth of the epistemological break which I propose for examination. I suspect that it goes deeper than the breaks suggested by Freud — and it is certainly more directly related to the subject with which educators deal.

Only after several years of research on the history of the conceptual space which emerged in archaic Greece did I grasp the depth to which the computer-as-metaphor exiles anyone who accepts it — far from the space of the literate mind. I then began to reflect on the emergence of a new mental space whose generating axioms are no longer based on the encoding of speech sounds through alphabetic notation, but rather on the power to store and manipulate 'information' in bytes.

I do not propose that we examine the effects which the computer as a technical tool has on the keeping of and access to written records; nor how it can be used for teaching 'the three R's.' Further, I do not ask for a study on the traces the computer leaves on modern style and compositions. Rather, I call for reflection on a web of terms and ideas which connects a new set of concepts whose common metaphor is the computer, and which does not seem to fit into the space of literacy, where pedagogics originally took shape.

In calling for such attention I want to avoid the temptation to assign any causal function to the electronic machine. Just as those historians made a major mistake who maintained that the printing press was necessary to have the Western mind molded by 'linear thought,' so it would be a mistake to believe that the computer itself threatens the survival of the literate mind. A combination of small techniques in the scriptoria of twelfth-century monasteries created the visible text in which a very complex evolution of literate lifestyles and imagery found its appropriate mirror, centuries before Gutenberg cut his first font. And I suspect that a future historian will see the relationship between the computer and the waning of literate space in a similar way. Under circumstances much too complex even to suggest, at the height of economic and educational development — during the second quarter of the twentieth century — the web of literate axioms was weakened, and a new mental space or 'structure' found its metaphor in the Turing Machine. It would be unwise, in this plea, to propose how this new break should be studied. But by recalling a story told by Orwell I hope to make it plausible that the exploration of the break we are witnessing is central to the concern of any research on what 'education' might be about.

It is important to remember that, at the time Orwell worked on *1984*, the language of role theory which Mead, Linton and Murdock had coined in 1932 was just being picked up by sociology. The vocabulary of cybernetics was still confined to the lab. Orwell as a novelist sensed the mood of the time and invented the parable for a mind-set whose elements were as yet unnamed. He reflected on the effects which the treatment of speech as communication would have on people before the computer was available to model it on. In 1945 Western Union placed an ad in the *New York Times* seeking to employ 'communications carriers,' an euphemistic neologism for messenger boys. The Oxford English Dictionary Supplement gives this instance as the first use of the term with its current meaning.

Thus, Orwell's Newspeak is much more than a caricature of propaganda, or a parody of Basic English — which in the thirties had fascinated him for a while. Newspeak, at the end of the novel, is for him the cipher for something which then had no English equivalent. This becomes clear in the scene where O'Brien from the Thought Police says to Smith whom he tortures: 'We do not merely destroy our enemies, we change them [. . .] we convert, we shape them [. . .] we make our enemy one of ourselves before we kill him [. . .] we make his brain perfect before we blow it out [. . .]' At this point Smith, the novel's anti-hero, still believes that what O'Brien says must make sense to the listener. The next pages then describe how Smith is disabused of his literate mind. He will have to accept that O'Brien's world is both senseless and selfless, and that the therapy he undergoes has the purpose of making him join it.

Winston Smith works at the Ministry of Truth. He specializes in the abuse of language: propaganda in a caricature of Basic English. He practices extreme distortions that are possible within the literate mind. O'Brien has the task of leading him into an entirely new world, a space which Smith must first 'understand' and then accept. O'Brien says to him, 'Tell me why we cling to power [. . .] speak'! Strapped, Winston answers, 'you rule over us for our own good [. . .] you believe that human beings are not fit to govern themselves [. . .].' This answer would have pleased Ivan's Inquisitor in Dostoyevsky's novel, but it makes O'Brien turn the pain up to '33 degrees.' 'We seek power entirely for its own sake.' O'Brien insists that the State *is* power, and he has previously made Smith understand that this power consists in the ability to write *the* book. Winston is to be a line in that book, written or re-written by the State. 'Power is in tearing human minds to pieces,' says O'Brien, 'and putting them together again in new shapes of our own choosing.' Torture forces Winston to abandon his belief that Newspeak is a degraded form of English; he 'understands' that Newspeak is an exchange of meaningless know-how, without any *why* and without any *I*. When O'Brien holds up four fingers and calls them 'three,' Winston is to understand the message, not the speaker. At a loss for an English word for the exchange of message units between machines, Orwell calls the intended relationship 'collective solipsism.' Without knowing the appropriate word, namely, 'communication,' Winston has come to understand the world in which O'Brien's state operates. Orwell insists that the mere understanding of this world is not enough, it must be accepted.

To accept his existence without sense and self, Winston needs the ultimate therapy of 'Room 101.' Only after the betrayal there does he take himself for granted as part of 'a fantasy world in which things happen as they should' — namely, on a screen. And to accept being just a message unit of senseless power, Winston has first to erase his own self. Neither violence nor pain could break what Orwell calls his 'decency.' To become self-less like O'Brien, Winston must first betray his last love, Julia (in room 101). Later, when the two former lovers meet as burned-out shells, they know that in Room 101 they had meant what they said. Self-betrayal in face of the rats was the last thing Winston *meant*. According to Orwell, only this kind of betrayal could integrate the victim into the executioner's solipsistic system of meaningless communication.

I have now recounted the fable. It is a story of the State that has turned into a computer, and that of educators who program people so that they come to lose that 'distality' between *self* and *I* which had come to flower within literate space. They learn to refer to themselves as 'my system,' and 'to input' themselves as appropriate lines into a mega-text. In the novel, Orwell speaks tongue-in-cheek. He tells more than a cautionary tale, but he does not portray something he believes could ever come to be. He creates the cipher for the State that survives society; communication between role players that survives the literate mind; 'people' who remain after the betrayal of decency. *1984* is for Orwell the cipher of something impossible which his journalistic genius made appear imminent.

In retrospect, Orwell appears to some of us as an optimist. He believed that the cybernetic mind would spread only as a result of intensive instruction. In fact, many people now unthinkingly accept the computer as the key metaphor for themselves and for their place in the world, without any need for 'Room 101.' They quietly and uncomplainingly cross over from the mental domain of lay literacy to that of the computer. And they do so often with as little competence in the use of the machine as thirteenth-century laymen had in the use of pen and parchment. The cybernetic mind engulfs a new kind of layman without assistance from educational agencies. This is the reason why at the outset I called attention to two rarely formulated questions: first, is there any reason to believe that the new intense concern of the educational establishment with universal *clerical* literacy can, in fact, strengthen and spread the literate mind? And, second, has schooling now become an initiation ritual introducing students to the cybernetic mind by hiding from all its participants the contradiction between the literate ideas education pretends to serve and the computer image it sells?

With these suggestions I hope to have clarified the subject

and argued the urgency of the research for which I plead. This research is based on historical phenomenology of assumptions about speech. Only the technique of the alphabet allows us to record speech and to conceive of this record — in the alphabet — as 'language' that we *use* in speaking. A certain view of the past and of bringing up the young is determined by this assumption. The research I call for could set out to identify the assumptions which are characteristic and proper to 'education' only within this mental space.

The research would further explore the degree to which literates and illiterates alike share the special mind-set which arises in a society that uses alphabetic record. It would recognize that the literate mind constitutes a historical oddity of seventh century B.C. origin. It would further explore this space which is uniform in its characteristics, but diverse in all the distortions and transformations these permit. Finally, this research will recognize the heteronomy of the literate space in regard to three other domains: the worlds of orality, those shaped by non-alphabetic notations and, finally, that of the cybernetic mind.

You can see that my world is that of literacy. I am at home only on the island of the alphabet. I share this island with many who can neither read nor write, but whose mind-set is fundamentally literate like mine. And they are threatened, as I am, by the betrayal of those clerics who dissolve the words of the book into just a communication code.

Mnemosyne: The Mold of Memory

'The Object of Objects: An Elegy for the Anchored Text'.
Concluding Statement at an International Conference on
'The Socio-Semiotics of Objects: The Role of Artifacts in
Social Symbolic Processes'
University of Toronto, 24th June, 1990

Modes of pastness

We all have the power to recall what has been. Each one
shares with his own generation the ability to recreate the
past. Life in the shadow of pastness is what makes us human.
However, in several ways people differ because of the
different pasts they have.

Each of us can remember his own past. But the older I get
the more I treasure the discrepancies between what is
uniquely mine in the past and that which others can share
with me. The past that appears in this interstice is that past
which can surprise me. For even when we have grown up
together and later on recall the same moment that we lived
together, my substance that is recalled is frequently not
yours. And, further, the chords which the past strikes when it
comes to me might jar those that respond in your heart. Only
years later I suddenly grasped that when those bells tolled
for the wedding, for you they meant death. This is one reason
why I like to reminisce with others: the shoddy evening that
made me cringe when I thought of it has put on a festive
dress since you told me about it.

When the past is invoked it always comes in a different
dress. And each time it passes it leaves something new

behind, it deposits a freshly-spun layer on the cocoon which I take for my memories. Whenever I take a glass of Burgundy, that memorable afternoon with my brother returns, but with a new coloring.

This diversity of the 'same' past is so fascinating and adventurous that it could almost blind us to yet another, even more fundamental difference between past and past. The past returns in quite distinct modes of pastness, according to the historical epoch into which it is called. '*Les neiges d'antan*' refer to a past which is incomparable to that of 'the old clock on the staircase.'

Several of these modes of pastness I have to know by experience. When I enter a church — be it Greek or Latin — I know that I am in a temple erected above an empty tomb. The absence of the saint during the Liturgy is of a different kind than the absence of Charlemagne when I discuss his treasures with a colleague in an office. Thanks to my upbringing, I have a spontaneous albeit faint sense of the difference between liturgical and academic remembrance. And I have lived long enough in a Mexican village to sense how the newly-dead come back on 2nd November, walking along the lines of flower petals that show them the way from the grave to their erstwhile home. In spite of the goose pimples, I know that they do not come to be with me.

Other modes of pastness lie completely beyond the range of my feelings. I know about them only by hearsay. My body is dumb to the chords they seem to strike in others. Conceptually, I can refer to the experience that befits the re-presentation of African ancestors or the mythical return of Mexican gods. But the world into which I was born and in which I was raised has blotted out the reality of the ambience in which these events can take place. And the more I reflect upon historical reports about remembrance, the better I come to see that there is a chasm which separates the past now and then.

Culture as mnemosyne

The present is the mold of the past. What Boas called a

culture I, following the advice of Aby Warburg, could just as well call *mnemosyne*. What else is culture but the frame within which the shadows come back and are enfleshed? Thus understood, the customs and symbols, the rituals and artifacts of a culture can be imagined as one body that resonates when the past emerges. Like the wave patterns that form in a body of water when it is touched by a breeze, culture-as-*mnemosyne* is affected as a whole by the winds from its own beyond. But just as the waves across a body of water begin to mumble and spray when they hit a cliff or the shore, so there are within each culture coastlines against which memory breaks.

Different ages have used different devices to conjure up what has been: Greeks used the lyre, Aztecs the flute, Bushmen the drum, to make the whole body of *mnemosyne* resonate to the rhythms of the past. Beads and knots, paintings and marked paths through mountains and deserts, have all been pressed into service for initiation into the past. Franks used notched sticks to recount the exact number of magical words needed for the oath. The Bards had their own techniques, useless to the literate. The Yorubas used masks in dances, Christians assemblies above an empty grave.

Script as a bridge

Some societies adopted script as a privileged route into the past. But script is not just a path over which shades can come; it is a bridge for messages that have been left, a bridge that spans a chasm into the beyond. Or, it is like a vessel that ferries memories that have been recorded by the dead. But script is not the main material of cultural memories, even in most of those societies where it plays a prominent role. On this point also, contemporary, post-typewriter society is arguably a major exception. Many conceive and perceive their memories, waking or sleeping, as floating, unattached 'texts.'

The scripts of the past can be studied with different intents. For the archaeologist the script itself is an object that survives from the past. For the historian, the script is a vehicle which allows him to recover the events or perceptions that the document was meant to record. For the student of pastness itself, the script has a more specific function. For him, the script is a privileged object which allows him to explore two things: the mode of recall used in a given epoch, and also the image held by that epoch about the nature of memory and therefore of the past.

On the present occasion I want to pursue one very special aspect of script, and ask what it can tell me about an epoch's perception of pastness. I want to limit myself to the patterning of the surface by the use of letters, and to the effect that this patterning has on the epoch's conception of 'memory.' In other words, I want to examine the power of the pattern of impagination to signify the mode of recall rather than the subject that is recalled through the content of the written.

My subject is impagination as the mold of memory. In any mold I can distinguish two things: I can ask if the coin will be molded round or oval-shaped, small or large, flat or convex, *and* I can ask whom it will represent, King Pippin or Charlemagne. Here I want to focus on the page in the first sense.

I have no doubt that in different epochs the patterning of the writing surface has molded the concept of what memory is all about. I cannot prove this here; I can only make it plausible by examining a very special instance, namely, the writing surface which took the form of a book-page. I believe that during the twelfth century the page changed its molding function, that a number of technical changes, all affecting the arrangement of letters at this particular moment, made out of the manuscript page a tool that transformed the notion of memory. Though subtle, these changes had a powerful social effect. And they occurred three hundred years before move-able type came into use. They supported a new set of axioms for the obvious, without which Gutenberg and Luther, Leibnitz and Descartes, *The New York Review of Books* and Penguin Books could never have become what they are.

The end of the old past in the twelfth century

I will organize my discourse around the writings of a twelfth-century author, Hugh of Saint-Victor. He was an Augustinian Canon Regular born in Flanders around 1100 and brought up in Thuringia. He came to Paris at the time when Abelard began his lectures on method, and the Gothic arches of St Denis were abuilding, when Peter the Venerable brought the Koran from Toledo to translate it, and the first troubadours were composing vernacular songs. He died as head of the School of Saint-Victor. Hugh left a vast opus, and three of his books are particularly suited to show up the historic seam that runs through his relationship with the page. I will comment on the perception of memory in these three books.

The first is the *Didascalicon*, subtitled, *de arte legendi*. It is the first book to make the 'art of reading' into the subject of a treatise. The explicit contents of the book have often been examined. I have read it, listening to what Hugh implies in answer to two of my questions: what did he do when he 'read'? And what did he imagine he was doing? What was the precise activity of his hands, mouth, tongue, eyes and ears when he read? And what was the meaning that he gave to lines, words, parchment, ink and whatever else was there, in front of him, on the page? I read the *Didascalicon* to find out about Hugh's reading rather than about the substance of his teaching on the seven arts. I did so to become sensitive to the ethology of learning in his time.

As I read Hugh, I felt invited to start out on a pilgrimage through the pages. I ambulate with him through the espalier of lines on which words are strung up like grapes which I can pick, and from which I am urged to suck the tasty sweetness of wisdom. Reading is presented to me as a kinetic activity, as a tasting, as a declamation that will become meaningful only if I open my ears. Of course, the eyes have their role. But it is not the role I attribute to my eyes when I read today. Hugh imagines his eyes as having a double function: they are a source of illumination, since their light makes words on the page sparkle, and they are windows that let in the light of wisdom which shines through the pages.

The second book by Hugh that I want to examine is very short. Today we might call it a hand-out for class. It is titled *De tribus maximis circumstantiis* and is a manual for pre-teen novices who need elementary instruction on the art of learning by rote. Surprisingly, its text lay unacknowledged for many centuries, and the first printed edition appeared in 1932. Though this pamphlet is tiny, it is of great originality.

Since Greco-Roman antiquity one of the first things a student had to learn was the art of memory. Until the beginning of the twentieth century, memorization remained one of the basic skills a student of the humanities had to cultivate. Only during the last several decades has it gone out of style. In antiquity, the student usually followed the method Cicero describes. He was trained to construct a mental 'palace,' a fantasized dwelling with many rooms. He had to label those passages he wanted to remember with an emblem, for instance a red apple, and place several such marked phrases in one of these imagined rooms if he wanted to have them present at the same point of a debate. Within the confines of this palace, the pupil acquired the skill to dash with agility from one room to another; he learned to be prompt in finding the sentences he had prepared for use in examinations at school or under cross-examination in court.

In *De tribus*, Hugh places himself in the tradition of memory training. However, Hugh's novice is warned not to be jumpy. His memory is not being trained for legal attack and defence but for contemplative penetration of Holy Scripture. He learns to stay firm in one place, as if he were in the choir stall of a Gothic cathedral surrounded by several dozen multicolored frames:

> My child, Wisdom is a treasure, and thy heart is the place where you want to keep it [. . .] there are distinct hiding places for gold, for silver, for gems. You must come to know these different places to recover what you have hidden in them. You must become like the money changer at the fair whose hands speedily move from one satchel to the other, always reaching for the right coin.

This patient and restful fixation of the learner in his proper place is for Hugh an equivalent to the grounding of wisdom. '*Confusion* is the mother of ignorance and forgetfulness. *Discretion* makes intelligence shiny and memory strong.' The pupil is to place his right foot on the beginning of an imaginary line, onto which he will then mark a sequence of Roman numerals running all the way to the horizon. Each one of these discrete numerals from I to beyond XLVIII will then serve the learner as a kind of ledge onto which he can place a concept or an arbitrary visual symbol that labels it. On one of these 'ladders' he might list all the rivers that appear in the Bible: the four that flow forth from Paradise, the four that the Israelites had to cross, and the four that water the Holy Land. On another ladder the virtues or the Angels or the Apostles might find their place. While the right foot of the novice keeps all the lines converging, he will reach out, like the money changer at the fair, to recover what he has learned.

The third work I want to examine is much larger and made up of two volumes. It contains a complete set of rules for the construction of Noah's Ark in the pupil's heart. It is not meant for novices, but for mature Brothers, although what seems to be taken for granted in his circle would today stamp one as a freak, as a performer in a circus. In the same way in which Noah saved the animals during the flood, the pupil will preserve his memories in the midst of the sinful world's violent storms. In detail, Hugh describes how this ark is to be built: as a many-tiered floating box, with staircases and ladders, rafters and spars. This imaginary raft serves Hugh as an immense three-dimensional bulletin board. The mast and rudder, each separate part of each door frame, is present to him in every detail. And to each of these structural elements he has attached a memory of a thing. Whatever juicy morsel he has picked up on his pilgrimage through the pages of a book has been pinned by him to a spot of the ark to which he can reach out when he meditates in the dark. With his adult pupils he insists that the monk has left his abode on earth; that he sails through *historia* with *historia*'s model — the Ark of Noah — floating in his heart. If Hugh's

Ark were unfolded as a blueprint, with the labels a readable size, a parchment covering a classroom would be needed to print everything he attached to his structure.

Memoria is dying like the forest

I have tried repeatedly to read from these three books to the students I teach at the University of Pennsylvania. Each time one or two, really puzzled, began to compare their own certainties with those of Hugh. But most spent the semester attempting to evade the necessity of facing an age when people did all the remembering rather than leaving the job to machines. They belong to a generation which accepts not only the disappearance of forests, but of *memoria* as well. One forestry student suggested an analogy: yes, forests are dying. But haven't virgin forests died out long ago? Why shouldn't mixed forests go the same way to extinction? Tree farming will be in, and laws will make sure that there are playgrounds in the farms. This will bring children much closer to nature than hazardous forests now permit.

When my students open a book, they do not set out on a pilgrimage. In the age of the tape recorder it has become hard to convince any of them to memorize a list of dates. And rare are those colleagues who were privileged to have had a teacher of rhetoric who trained their ability of recall. Memory, when I discuss it with most, has something to do with rote and megabytes, or archetypes and dreams. For them, the page as a *pagus* — a cultured expanse of fields and buildings that invite one for a walk — it is a romantic fantasy or an escape from the unconscious, not the other side of reality, as it is for Hugh. Even stranger seems the construction of a life-boat for History in the heart.

Not just two sets of incomparable metaphors, but two mental topologies separate Hugh's world from ours. Two kinds of pages act here as mirrors, as metaphors, and also as co-generators of two distinct mental spaces. I know of no better way to clarify the distance between such heterogeneous mental spaces than an examination of the respective *pages*. The page layout can be examined as a mirror of the epochal *Weltanschauung*, but also as its mold.

Comparison of three 'pages'

To do so I want to compare not just two but three types of pages: the *pagina* through which Hugh imagines himself moving, the *text* which has been familiar to students from the thirteenth to the late twentieth century, and the electronic shadow of a digitalized *document file* that *Wordperfect* or *Wordstar* now enable me to manage on the screen.

Within the last two decades, 'text' has acquired a new and vague meaning not only in philosophy and science, but also in ordinary speech. It can refer to a paragraph written in English, a program written in *Pascal*, a characteristic sequence of amino-bases in a *gene*, or the sequence of tones in a bird song. Having been brought up on a mixed fare of Biblical exegesis and Karl Kraus, Gide and Mencken, it took me some time in the early sixties to adapt to the new uses of this word in ordinary speech. I still remember how I first noticed this spillover from structuralist and biological usage into the meaning of text, at the time when English departments became part of the 'school of communications.' In 1970, more out of loyalty than out of conviction, I agreed to write a foreword for a colleague's book. When the publisher sent the finished product, I was disturbed by the fact that the 'text' of his essay had been radically changed since I had written the foreword. I was upset by this lack of respect for the written word. At a party, more than a decade later, I again ran into the author. I wanted to know what he was doing now. I was a guest in his department, and by 'doing' I of course meant 'writing.' 'Fantastic things,' was his reply. 'I have bought a text composer and you cannot imagine what kinds of things it can do. I fed *our* book into it, and it gives me finally a fully satisfactory text.' I was not just shocked but offended as I saw a 'text' cut loose from any page.

Until that moment I had not been aware to what degree I had sanctified the text, to what depth I am beholden to its inviolability. I just cannot extricate myself from its tissue. Unlike Augustine or Hugh, I have been born into a macro-epoch of Western history during which text-derived notions define society, nature and ego. I am not an old rabbi or monk whose home is *in* the sacred object, who can meander through the book as if it were a valley or desert. I live among copies, articles, and critical editions. I am, through and through, a child of a post-medieval world in which every-thing which is perceived is also fatally *described*. My eyes do not wander, they take in the text. I voice and I hear the text that I have taken in. In Hugh's time, when a cow changed owners, an oath ended the transaction; one hand on the cow's rump and the other on beard or balls while audible words made the sale. A hundred years later already, the exchange was likely to result in a writ. What confirmed it was not an action but an object which *describes* the animal and the two parties. The nexus of thing to persons was no longer sworn-to possession but certified holding. Truth came to be embodied in protocols.

This is the world into which I was born. This makes me increasingly into a has-been, a stranger in the new world of homeless text that appears for editing, ghostlike on the screen.

The end of bookishness

George Steiner has given a name to the self-image that results from being born into the text. He calls them 'bookish' people. According to Steiner, bookishness is a historical singularity, a mental climate which results from a unique coincidence of technique, ideology and social texture. It depends on the possibility to own books, to read them in silence, to discuss them *ad libitum* in echo chambers like academies or coffee shops or periodicals. This kind of relationship to the text has been the ideal of schools. Paradoxically, however, the more schools became compul-sory for a majority, the smaller became the percentage of people who are bookish in this sense. For most people born into the middle of the twentieth century, schooling prepared for the text on the screen.

For Steiner, bookishness comes with print. While I find his phenomenology of bookishness admirable, I argue that the unique bookish character of Western perception is older than the technique of printing with moveable characters. In my opinion, bookishness comes into existence when the visible text undergoes a mutation, when it begins to float above the page and, 300 years before printing, its shadow can appear here and there, in this or that book, on parchment or in the 'soul.' This happened at the time of Hugh's death, two generations before universities were founded. The text itself became a pilgrim that could come to rest here and there. It became a ship laden with goods which could anchor in any harbor. But it could not be read, its treasures could not be unloaded, unless it had come to rest at a pier. I am amazed but not ashamed to notice how deeply I am marked by this bookish sense for the text.

And I am certainly not alone. An almost trivial experience confirms it. Living as I do on the fringes of institutions, one thing I had to give up long ago was the stenographer. When I was in my twenties and thirties it seemed obvious that I could call someone and dictate. This is how much writing has been done since the art was invented. Then came the dictaphone and, later, the computer. Stenographers became rare treasures, secretaries became expensive, typists mere operators of text-managing machines, while editors called for floppies. For people who are not in the organization, it became mandatory to type what they had penned, and this meant to learn to use the computer. Under these circumstances, I have had the opportunity to teach this minimal skill to almost half a dozen of my closest associates. The machine, after all, works like a typewriter for people with weak fingers, to which a few functions are added. And the first function the newcomer must learn is 'DELETE.' I have observed how six people, all of them learned readers, reacted to their first encounter with the delete key: all were upset, two actually became sick. The disappearance of a blocked sentence, and the closing of the gap by an onrush of words, were experienced by each of them as something offensive. This is not how we forget, nor is the command 'RESTORE' an analog to how we remember. For a bookish mind there is something deeply disturbing in the way in which the terminology of humanist criticism is appropriated by the programmer of machine commands. What appears on the screen is not *written*. It is writing as little as Magritte's 'pipe' is a pipe.

When I sit in front of the computer screen, I face an object which is beyond the horizon established by alphabetic literacy. Hieroglyphics and Maya codices are beyond the skyline of letters. But, historically speaking, these antiques — like Assyrian clay tablets, pyramid texts and Maya bark codices — are out of my inner line of vision, they lie beyond the horizon in back of me. They are models of bridges into the past of another time, as distant from my text as the George Washington Bridge is from the lianas that Incas plaited across the canyons of the Andes. What I face, what lies in front of me, is a flood of programmed arrangements that train me to select, retrieve, block, insert, delete, save, restore, merge, release and go to, to toggle on and off between files that are neither present nor absent. And when I have spent a sufficient number of hours in front of the screen, it has an effect on me. It takes some time for my eyes to readapt themselves to the adobe walls and ceiling beams of the room in which I sit. It requires an effort to discard the tool kit of cybernetic concepts that I used to transfer my *manu scriptum* into a computer file.

To recall means to let things appear, to let them emerge from below the surface of the water, to allow them to step out of the mist. It also means to turn around and look backward with longing eyes, straining the ear to pick up a tune that has become faint. It means to raise the dead by conjuring up their shadows. All these metaphors work when I re-call and re-dress the forgotten. But this is not what I do as a historian of the page. My intent here is the recovery of a past mode of pastness. I want to recover the page as it looked for Hugh of Saint-Victor. I want to gain understanding of the way in which the page brought the past back for him. His *memoria*, and not what memory has become in the age of computers, is the subject of my inquiry. And to come close to this subject I need a discipline which keeps me alert to my own way of looking, while I interpret his writings about the *ars legendi*.

Kuchenbuch's crab

In the search for a historiographic discipline which recovers the past without ever forgetting its distance from the present, Ludolf Kuchenbuch has found a parable. He speaks of historiography through the eyes of a crab. Most animals get away by turning around, and facing ahead. The crab moves backward, while its popping eyes remain fixed to the object they flee. The screen is my image for the present. Phoenician, Hebrew, cuneiform and hieroglyphic script are back there, out of my reach. I want to explore what happens if I begin to move backwards, with my eyes fixed on the present. And during a first stage of such a blind trip into the past, what gets between me and the screen are things I recall from my own past experience.

As I move away from the screen onto which my eyes remained fastened, the first stop I make is in Cornell. I cannot forget the occasion, the night Che Guevara was killed. I was there to study the archives of Myron Stykos who — with a huge grant from the Ford Foundation — had gathered thousands of Latin American editorials dealing with birth control. He wanted to classify the reasons for which people approved or disapproved. I wanted to use the same material to find out what coil, spiral and pill and condom meant. With his economic resources, Stykos had even then been able to use a computer. For a whole night I re-programmed it, straining my limited knowledge of Fortran. This was my first encounter with the machine. If I now remember the sleepless night alone in the lab and the later conversations with engineers, one thing becomes clear to me: then, twenty-five years back, anything approaching the text composer I now take for granted was not utopian, but it certainly was not something commonly envisaged. No doubt, information theory had already begun to drench common talk. Systems analysis had begun to enter hard and social sciences. Cybernetic terminology had come into fashion in the Academy. But in newspapers, any use of these new words was frankly mystifying if they were not somehow explained.

Had I gotten up from the work station, turned around and, in my memory, walked back to the mid-sixties, almost inevitably I would have kept on those special glasses I wear to type my manuscript into *Wordperfect*. I would have moved back through the books I have read since then, from Penrose or Moravec or both the late and earlier writings of Chomsky, and to the first encounters with Förster or his pupils Varela and Maturana. I would have focused my attention on how I came slowly to see things as I see them now. I would have assembled materials for the socio-genesis of my current concepts and percepts. But by moving back in a crab-like manner, my main attention is drawn to how my world was then. My discipline consists in remembering the surprise as its elements were shattered or dissolved. I try not to look at a past moment with foresight, but to know the present with crab-like hindsight. In the mid-sixties, text, though no longer bookish, was still essentially related to paper and print.

As I move about ten years further back, into the late fifties, the screen goes out of sight. Only a pale glitter above my mental horizon indicates the *work station* from which I have moved back. At the University, no one seriously thought of a Department of Communications. I remember an evening with visiting biologists in a seafood restaurant on the south coast of Puerto Rico. These colleagues had come for a conference on genetics and spoke about information that was textually encoded in genes. I understood what they were saying: the analogies between message-strings and biological variations were striking. But there was from the beginning something uncanny for a medievalist: did these people really speak of a submicroscopic text in the book of nature? Whom did this eerie text address? It took me years to sort out the mental discomfort caused to me by the necessity of accepting this novel metaphor. It was obvious that these biologists used 'text' for a sequence of characters which no one had written, no one was meant to understand, no one was meant to interpret. They spoke of 'writing' and 'reading' as functions performed by things, not by people.

As I reflect on these two first stations in my crab-like crawling through landscapes of past innocence, I am tempted to stop at the next station: my first encounter with the idea that language can be studied as a code. Remembering my own mental framework in the late forties, and reminding my colleagues of theirs, I would have a sufficient distance from the present to describe and then analyze the gulf between the mental space then and now. If I did this, my main attention would be drawn to the way in which the existence of the new use of text has affected the popular mind rather than technical or scientific discourse. The symbolic impact of suggestive things, like 'the' computer, that act as sacred symbols, and the symbolic impact of conjuring words, like 'the' text, would hold my main interest. But at this time I only want to create the proper mood for such an analysis. I want to achieve this by going back to the rather distant past when a new technology had a faintly comparable effect. By pointing out the great difficulties faced by the historian in interpreting the change of the page in 1200 A.D., I hope to enliven the courage of those who focus on the recent past. To throw light on what I see as the end of the era of bookish reading, I want to look at its beginning and again, in crab-like fashion, move back to the time just before the University came into existence.

Walter Benjamin has invented the seductive image of the 'Angel of History.' He looks back and faces the gale of time that rushes him backward into the present. And before this angel's steadfast eyes, the wreckage of time stretches out. As a crab, I move in the exact opposite way. While the present from which I come remains steadily in front of me, one after the other of my own certainties disappears from the landscape through which I move back. About the time the Romanesque atria were replaced by Gothic portals, my back collides with a door which opens as I move beyond it and stop. This is the moment which Richard Southern calls a hinge-time into European or Modern times, but which I prefer to see as the turning of a page. In fact, I like to imagine that the door which my crab's rump has moved is a manuscript page — this allows me to continue my day-dream. In the Romanesque cloister in which I have come to a stop, I can see two objects in front of me: the door that has opened inwards, and next to it many other pages of a previous time. And through the door opening in the very far distance I can still see a faint glint of neon. Keeping myself with much discipline in the crab's posture, I continue to face two 'texts' which lie in the beyond, while I examine Hugh's *pagina* which fits the age in which I have arrived. This discipline might help to distance both electronic and bookish categories from the text I am now examining.

Hugh's book begins with the sentence that reading is a search, a kind of pilgrimage. It is seeking light that will enlighten his eyes. As I read him, I can see him in the choir, patiently waiting for the dawn to reveal the scenes of the stained glass. Words still light up; they each have their own luminosity, like the figures in the epoch's miniatures painted on gold ground. Painted light, which by the time of the early printing press begins to strike the figures of Renaissance artists, is not of his time. Thomas Aquinas, in the thirteenth century, can already conceive it when he speaks of *lumen formale sub quo* as something which we might call the 'per-spective of a discipline.' No, Hugh wants to implant self-igniting words in the hearts of his pupils. He wants his students to memorize treasures. When placed where they belong, words can be woven, textured into *historia*. When well memorized, words illuminate each other mutually in the analogies of their meaning.

Whatever survived the wrath of the Creator against a humankind that got mixed up with the giants was assigned its place on the Ark of Noah. The book can thus be seen as an Ark. The heart then contains a book. The twelfth century is rich in ways to inculcate this point. We must guard what we let into the heart to preserve it from stains. Before using the brush, the heart's surface should be softened so that the ink imbibes the substance. No one should be able to erase these traits. They should be as firm as on a parchment on which the penknife cannot dig out what has been written without creating a hole. The colors should be layed on in several coats, well polished to make them glitter.

Arca means both barge and chest. It's a vessel for objects like words. Almost tasteless is the external book, *modi cum sapita est lectio, nisi glossam sumat ex corde*, unless it gets its sound (or just as well translated, 'its tongue') from the heart. What Hugh picks up on his way through the lines can be heard by his ear and tasted by his mouth. His lips bring out the sound of the pages, *voces paginarum*, as if they were the strings of a lyre. In Hugh's writings the sharp line between things and words that some of his contemporaries try to draw is still very fuzzy. He reads orally, describing the sensation this leaves on lips and tongue: sweetness sweeter than honey. Hugh stands at the end of a mumbling, meditative, degustatory, auditory tradition of reading that was initiated by the Church Fathers, especially Augustine. It would be a grave mistake to confuse the *memoria* cultivated by this monkish, liturgical reading with that other, classical *memoria* that was fostered by Roman rhetoric teachers who prepared politicians and lawyers, training them to use words in harangues and arguments. Only when medieval *memoria* is understood in contrast to Ciceronian precepts will its end, around 1200, be properly understood.

Hugh is the first author I know who looks beyond his own epoch of reading; he distinguishes three kinds of reading, namely, for my own ears, for those of my listeners and that which is done by silent contemplation of the page. How he did this third kind of reading remains a mystery to me as I sit, like a crab, looking both at the page from the next century, that has opened as a door into my line of vision, and — in contrast to it — at those pages which were written before Hugh's death in 1142. The early and high medieval page is not meant to be absorbed by mere looking. It calls for kinesthetic decipherment. Glosses invade the interlinear space. One page looks like the next. Paragraphs are rare. Titles give little help. You can go back to a physical spot in the book where the sentence you remember will be found in this particular manuscript. But scribal techniques do almost nothing to help your visual orientation within a 'text.' I cannot help imagining that the *pagina* Hugh contemplated in silence was an ark floating in his heart rather than an object before his exterior eyes. He knew into which of its rooms to move, above which door to look at a lintel to find the sentence he had attached there.

This is completely different when I look at a page one hundred years younger. The page has become the support for a graphically articulated text. The page is no longer a storage place for objects, nor an espalier of word-bearing vines. The carefully articulated page on the backturned door that faces me, results from the fusion of a dozen technical innovations. What would have startled Hugh are paragraphs, indentures, numbering of arguments *ad primum . . . ad quintum*, the space between the lines that has been cleared of glosses. Stars or crockets refer to where the gloss fits. The main text is written in a larger script. The scribe must have calculated carefully how much of it fits on each page so the corresponding volume of marginal notes would still fit. Mercury red is used to mark quotations as distinct from the author's own words. On the first page I find a table of contents which refers to the chapter number, or even the verse. Titles and subtitles strike the eye. There might even be an index at the end of the book which lists not only names but also things in alphabetical order. The idea of ordering things by the first letter of the corresponding word would have struck Hugh's generation as quirky. This is hard for us to grasp until we remember that we too would be maddened by a list of months, weekdays or street numbers in alphabetical order. But we also have difficulty keeping in mind how new random access was to a society in which reading was always a pilgrimage, a route meandering from here to there. The more I look at the two pages next to each other, the clearer I see here the birth of a visible something: a verbal texture fixed by writing to be taken in at a glance. The *text* can now be visualized, imagined, conceived as something which has real existence apart from its incarnation within these covers or those.

Moving counter to the Angel of History, I have reached

that point at which the text was born. The idea of the text is something comparable to the idea of the alphabet. Once the alphabet had been invented, it was there, one of those things which, once born, is mature — like the wheel, the horse collar, or the rudder placed into the axis of the ship. They cannot be significantly improved, but they can be used in totally unexpected ways. This is what happened to letters when they became the stuff from which visualized text was made. And since the text took off from the page, it has remained a powerful metaphor. And just as letters were the stuff out of which the new entity was then made, so the text has now become the stuff from which an entirely new set of concepts is derived.

In physics, Max Planck resurrected the metaphor of the world as a book and of the scientist as a 'reader' of nature. He compared the physicist to the archaeologist trying to make sense of the traces left by a totally alien culture that has neither the intent to reveal to, nor the desire to hide, something from the reader. The first to use writing no longer as a metaphor but as an explanatory analogy was also a physicist, the Jewish emigrant Erwin Schrodinger. From Dublin in 1943, he suggested that genetic substance could best be understood as a stable text whose occasional variations had to be interpreted as textual variations. As a physicist, Schrodinger stepped completely beyond his domain formulating this biological model. Only a few months later, the biologist Avery demonstrated for the first time that genomes could be 'inserted' into bacteria, almost like a gloss that slips into the manuscript's main text. Each individual at the moment of fertilization could now be visualized as an original text.

Schrodinger's idea affected the notion of text at least as deeply as the scribal revolution did around 1200. He brought into existence something new, a sequence of 'letters' that exercises power without coming from or addressing a mind. Since Schrodinger, 'text' is a meaningless and senseless program which acts as a determinant for the organization of a process.

The first person to have understood the extraordinary

semantic consequence of this re-formulation of text as authorless command not destined to be given meaning in the act of reading, is Erwin Chargaff. Celebrating the hundredth anniversary of the first isolation of 'nucleic acids', (by Miescher in 1869) Chargaff says that upon reading Schrodinger in the light of Avery's experiments 'though obscurely, I saw before me, in very rough lines, a "grammar" of biology.' Chargaff understood that by transforming Schrodinger's animistic analogy into an explanatory model, just four 'bases' — rather than a great variety of 'letters' — would be sufficient to encode the variability of living nature. It was also Chargaff who made me understand the two-fold symbolic consequence of the new language of biology. First, the nightmare of universal literacy is now being anchored in the ability of organic molecules 'to read' each other. Second, progress henceforth means that man re-programs the book of nature.

By this comment the crab has vaulted through the open door that separates Romanesque and Gothic pages and landed again in front of the computer.

Computer Literacy and the Cybernetic Dream

Lecture given at the Second National Science,
Technology and Society Conference on
'Technological Literacy' organized by
Science through Science, Technology and Society
project of Pennsylvania State University
Washington D.C., February 1987

Technological Literacy has been placed on the agenda for a second year at this meeting of educators, engineers and scientists. This year, the theme is technology and the imagination. Imagination works day and night. I want to speak about the imagination in daytime when people are immersed in neon lights. Only indirectly will I refer to that mini-competence on keyboards, at switches and in face of graphs which makes everyone feel a little bit of a hacker. As useful as it might be, I look at this kind of pseudo-literacy mainly as a condition to keep your sense of humor in a world that has been programmed. I will deal with the machine and its cybernetic logic only insofar as these induce a vaguely dream-like mental state. I am concerned about how to keep awake in the computer age.

It is helpful to distinguish three ways in which a technique affects the human condition. Technical means can be tools in the hand of the engineer. The engineer is faced with a task and for it selects, improves and applies a tool. In a second way, tools have a way of affecting social relations. A telephone-society engenders something new, still called 'trust' — toward people whom you address but cannot face. Finally, all tools tend to be themselves powerful metaphors which affect the mind. This is as true for the clock as it is for the motor or the engine; it is as true for the page covered with alphabetic signs as it is for a string of binary bits. The first two effects of tools, namely the technical use and its fallout on social structure, I want to bracket for today. I want to focus on cybernetics as a dominant metaphor, I want to speak of the computer as a potentially mind-boggling device.

However, before I get to this subject, I want to clarify one more point: I am not speaking about this ominous power of the computer in a general, world-wide, way. I am not saying what the computer as a metaphor does to Japanese children who have studied cangi-ideograms three hours daily for eleven years. I want to orient our discussion on the fit between the cybernetic metaphor and a particular mental state, the characteristically European, Western mental space which over a thousand years has been shaped by the alphabet and the alphabetic text as a dominant metaphor. I suggest this restriction for three reasons: first, because what I know about is mainly history; second, because I am studying the function of alphabetic notations, insofar as they have been considered as generators of post-medieval typically European unexamined axioms; and, thirdly, because I want to invite you to discuss with me the impact of the computer-as-metaphor not as a sociological, but as a literary and historical phenomenon.

Classical science has been created by people who recorded the sound of words by which they discussed nature. It was not created by Chinamen who for millennia have graphically expressed unsounding abstractions. Until recently natural scientists were, above all, literary men. Modern science therefore is an outgrowth of the literate mind, in the sense in which this term has been used by Milman Parry or Walter Ong. Turing's universal machine appears as a singularity within this mental space during that fateful year 1932/1933. I propose that we explore how the cybernetic metaphor proposed by Norbert Wiener has affected the mental topology of the alphabetic mind. I want to describe the disembodied mode of perception which corresponds to the computer-boggled mindstate in contrast to the perception characteristic of the literate mind.

For this mode of conceiving and communicating among people who are high on the cybernetic metaphor, Maurice Berman has coined an excellent term. He calls this state 'the cybernetic dream.' Many of you will know Berman from his 'Reenchantment of the World' published in 1981. He is now working on a new book, on the 'Body of History'. An article published in the *Journal of Humanistic Psychology* gives an attractive foretaste of what is to come.

Berman recognizes the dimming of those implicit certainties by which the classical literal mind had been shaped. He calls attention to many attempts to recognize alternative modes of consciousness and observation. Most of these — in one way or another — place themselves under the umbrella of 'New Age' and, according to Berman, most of them have one thing in common: they encourage their followers to abandon themselves to the cybernetic dream.

Berman, in this article, comes to this conclusion by examining a set of North American authors who have recently been influential in the general public and tend to pose as disenchanted scientists. He recognizes the enormous difference in language, logic and style between Douglas Hofstadter, Frank Capra and Ken Wilber, Jeremy Rifkin or Rupert Sheldrake. Deftly he sketches their respective pet-terms: holographic paradigms, morphogenetic fields, real time, implicate order. And convincingly he argues that all of them rush into the same trap into which even Bateson ended when he reduced the body — towards the end of his life — into part of a monistic, mental process.

All of these authors at one point claim to offer an epistemological approach to reality that would be an alternative to the mechanistic, empiricist, value-free consciousness which each one of these authors ascribes to 'current science' or 'the scientific establishment.' In fact, however, according to Berman, these authors do nothing of this kind. Each of them, albeit in different words, interconnects another set of concepts that are related to information theory and thus creates a purely formal, abstract, disembodied system of reference which he identifies with what is going on in his own mind. This state of mind, for Berman, is best called the 'cybernetic dream.' It puts the mind into a state which can be accommodated to any situation at all. For Berman, the cybernetic dream brings the logic of 300 years of mechanistic science to its full fruition. I would rather say: it represents a 'singularity' — in the sense in which a black hole is a singularity in time-space.

Berman tells the story of a friend called Susan. It so impressed me that I cannot but elaborate on it. Susan teaches high school in Northern Florida. Many of her students have home computers. When Susan assigns a paper to these students, they run off to their machines. They feed it Susan's key words, have it retrieve materials from data banks, string these together and present them to the teacher as their homework. One afternoon, Frank, one of these students, stayed on with Susan after class. The paper that week had been on drought and hunger south of the Sahara. Frank wanted to show her more of his printouts, and at one point Susan interrupted him. She said, 'Frank, tell me, what do you feel about this?' Frank stared at her for a moment and then replied: 'I don't know what you mean.' At this moment the abyss between Susan and Frank comes into view. Michel Foucault would have spoken about an epistemological chasm. Let me sketch her mind and his.

For Susan, a statement is an utterance; behind each utterance there is somebody who means what she says. And further, Susan cannot mean anything without feeling how this meaning is embodied. When she *spells out* 'hopeless hunger' she senses something, which she does not when she operates on '33.' Therefore, for Susan, the words that make up a sentence are like the planks of a bridge to the feelings of another.

For Frank, words are units of information that he strings together into a message. Their objective consistency and denotational precision, not their subjective connotates, count. He operates upon abstract notions and he programs the use of data. His perception is locked into his head. He controls redundancies and noise. Feelings and meanings would arouse anxiety, terror and surges of affection, and he keeps them low, he keeps his cool. The text composer is the model which imprints his mode of perception. He conceives of his senses as 'perceptors' and of his ego as a proprioceptor.

Susan (now taken as an ideal type) is a perceptually embodied self. Her utterances surge from the mass of flesh and blood, from the forest of feelings and meanings which engulf everything she has said. She is a teacher, because she has disciplined meanings and feelings without downgrading them. With great pains she has trained her inner Descartes and her inner Pascal to watch each other: to balance mind and body, spirit and flesh, logic and feeling.

Frank is, at this moment for me, the emblem of the opposite perceptual state. He has detached himself from the morass of feelings. He has learned how to take off, to leave the dense atmosphere behind and operate in free space, without gravity. He has hooked on to the computer and he has been caught in the dragnet of operational thinking. Turing's formula has induced for him the cybernetic dream. He can coast above the Sahel, view the parched Earth, the dying camel, and register growing despair and hostility. His mind is a camera which does not distort those signals it does not let in. He wants Susan to grade the takes that he has composed into a 'text.'

Susan and Frank are both persons. They are responsible for the mental state in which they are. Susan can steer her way between romantic sentimentality and critical lucidity, between sloppy and sensitive choice of connotates, choose the traditional lineage of authors into which she wants her metaphors to fit. When she speaks she is using words that have been written, and thinking for her is a way of silently spelling things out. This constant reference to the alphabet makes her different from the preliterate, but also in a very different way, from Frank. Frank, too, is responsible for what he does. He can use the cybernetic metaphor for what he does when he speaks as an analytic tool which misses more than it models. He can use it as a joke. Like Fromm when he speaks of psychic plumbing, Frank can refer to shit-in, shit-out. But he can also become sloppy and let this metaphor swallow all others, and finally move into the state Berman calls the cybernetic dream.

As the two mind-sets confront each other, both can harden into ideologies. I have known several Susans for whom literacy has become an anti-cybernetic ideology. They react to every reference to computers as fundamentalists react to communism. For these anti-computer fundamentalists a trip through computerland, and some fun with controls, is a necessary ingredient for sanity in this age. Those of you who study computer literacy sometimes forget its importance as a means of exorcism against the paralyzing spell the computer can cast. But I know many Franks who, under this spell, have turned into zombies, a danger Maurice Merleau-Ponty clearly foresaw almost thirty years ago. He then said — and I quote — that 'cyberneticism has become an ideology. In this ideology human creations are derived from natural information processes, which in turn have been conceived on the model of man-as-a-computer.' In this mind-state, science dreams up and 'constructs man and history on the basis of a few abstract indices' and for those who engage in this dreaming 'man in reality becomes that *manipulandum* which he takes himself to be.'

When I earlier described Susan and Frank standing opposite each other, separated by an epistemological chasm, I avoided saying that they 'face' each other. To speak with Merleau-Ponty, Susan's body is the 'soil of the sensible which emerges with every word and gesture,' and Frank's body is the defaced artifice of the 'information machine.' The two cannot face each other, and to 'interface', Frank would have to pick another of his own ilk.

When I think of the glazing which the screen brings out in the eyes of its user, my entrails rebel when somebody says that screen and eye are 'facing' each other. A verb for what happens there had not been coined when Merleau-Ponty wrote in 1959. The verb was created ten years later by McLuhan, and within a year 'to interface' was current in psychology, engineering, photography and linguistics. I hope that Susan is a friend who is seeking Frank's face. Perhaps Susan sees her vocation in seeking Frank's face.

PART FOUR

Twelve Years after *Medical Nemesis*:
A Plea for Body History

Consultation on 'Health and Healing in America'
Pennsylvania State University, January 1985

Twelve years ago I wrote *Medical Nemesis*. The book began with the statement: 'The medical establishment has become a major threat to health.' Hearing this today I would respond, 'so what'? Today's major pathogen is, I suspect, the pursuit of a healthy body. And, importantly, this endeavor has a history.

As a public cause, the pursuit first appears with the emergence of the nation state. People came to constitute a resource, a 'population.' Health became a qualitative norm for armies and then, during the nineteenth century, for workers; and later, for mothers. In Prussia, as in France, the medical police were charged with its enforcement. But the pursuit of health was also understood as a personal right, as the physical realization of the Jeffersonian right to the pursuit of happiness. The valetudinarian's dream of a ripe old age on the job, together with the economy's demand for productive workers and fertile reproducers, fused in the idea of health. But what began as a duty and entitlement has been transmogrified into a pressing need. In 1985, I would place the historical phenomenology of this novel need into the center of research. For many of our contemporaries, the pursuit of health has become consubstantial with the experience of their bodies.

Since I wrote *Medical Nemesis*, the symbolic character of health care has changed. Americans now pay more money to health professionals than they spend on either food or housing. An instructive paradox appears: medicines, psychologies, environments and social arrangements increasingly influence how people think and feel, while the concepts and theories to which the professions appeal are publicly questioned. As a result, expenditures on various and sundry programs of holistic well-being have increased faster than medical costs. Health appears to lie between the lines of every second advertisement, to be the inspiration of every other media image. Allocations for safety, ecology, law enforcement, education and civil defense are approved if they can be related to integral health care. Therefore the relative importance of the medical establishment within the health sector has been reduced. A curious mixture of opinionated and detailed self-care practices joined to a naive enthusiasm for sophisticated technology make the efforts and personal attention of physicians ever more frustrating. I suspect that the actual contribution of medicine to the pathogenic pursuit of health is a minor factor today.

In *Medical Nemesis*, I set out to examine the spectrum of effects generated by medical agents. I called these effects 'iatrogenic,' doing so with a rhetorical purpose. I wanted to call public attention to the research on medical effectiveness carried out during the late fifties and sixties. My conclusion stated the obvious: only a small percentage of all healing, relief from pain, rehabilitation, consolation and prevention was attributable to medicine. Most of these outcomes occur without or despite medical attention. Further, the iatrogenesis of disease is comparable in importance to the iatrogenesis of well-being. What sounded shocking then has now become commonplace. In his forecast for 1986, the US Secretary for Health estimates that 80 to 100,000 patients will be seriously injured by hospitalization. But this kind of accidental damage to individuals was marginal to the central argument of my book. I wrote in order to highlight the institutional, social, and cultural effects of the medical system. At the center of my analysis stood the iatrogenic reshaping of pain, disease, disability and dying, as these phenomena are experienced by their subject. The cultural constraints of these experiences and their symbolic impact, insofar as they are mediated by medicine, were my interest. I am not dissatisfied with my text, as far as it goes, but I am distressed that I was blind to a much more profound symbolic iatrogenic effect: the iatrogenesis of the body itself. I overlooked the degree to which, at mid-century, the experience of 'our bodies and our selves' had become the result of medical concepts and cares.

I did not recognize that, in addition to the perception of illness, disability, pain and death, the body-percept itself had become iatrogenic. Therefore, my analysis was deficient in two respects: I did not clarify the historical 'gestalt' of that period's body-percept or the role of medicine in shaping it. And since I was unaware of the iatrogenic nature of the experienced body, I did not explore its metamorphosis: the emergence of a body-percept congruent with a post-professional high-tech lifestyle. To gain perspective on such a contemporary metamorphosis, body history became for me an important condition for an examined life in the eighties.

I originally came to body history through teaching about the Middle Ages. In my courses on the twelfth century, I focus on the emergence of certain ideas, on themes and concepts for which antiquity has no true equivalents, but which in our time are experienced as certainties. One of these we call our 'selves.' 'Some thirty inches from my nose / the frontier of my person goes,' wrote W.H. Auden in one of his poems. If you are uncertain about this distinction between yourself and others, you cannot fit into Western society. There is general agreement that this sense of self emerges with the Crusades, cathedrals, European peasantry, and towns. Further, its successive forms and its contrast with different cultures have been well studied.

Little attention has been directed to the fact that the Western self is experienced as flesh and blood, that the birth of selfhood endowed Europe with a body of experience unlike any other. In collaboration with a colleague studying the early eighteenth-century body, I developed concepts necessary for a historical phenomenology of the body. And I soon met others struggling with the same questions in various periods and settings. As body history takes shape, we are able to understand how each historical moment is incarnated in an epoch-specific body. We now begin to decipher the body of subjective experience as a unique enfleshment of an age's ethos. Through these studies, I have learned to see the Western body as a progressive embodiment of self.

Searching for a common element which might help me interpret disparate changes in the transition from a Romanesque to a Gothic world view, I hit upon the notion of body history. I needed to explain how the odor of sanctity could disappear between 1110 and 1180, how relics came to heal on sight, the circumstances under which the bodies of the poor souls in Purgatory assumed their shapes. Why did the zoomorphs which decorate the inside of Romanesque churches become gargoyles poised for take-off on the outside of Gothic cathedrals? How did the Christ figure, with outstretched arms and clothed in royal raiment, become the naked, martyred body hanging on a cross by the year 1200? How to explain St Bernard training abbots for a thousand reformed Cistercian monasteries and teaching these men to breastfeed their young monks with the pure milk of Christ? And, most important, because of immense social conse-quences, I began to understand the context within which the ideas of modern sex and marriage were shaped. Men and women were endowed with 'human' bodies which each self could give to the other, thereby creating kinship ties between their respective families, not by the will of elders, but by a legal contract between individuals who exchange rights of the body.

I came to see that there was a distinct awareness of the body as the primary locus of experience. This body, specific to one period but subject to profound transformations some-times occurring within relatively short spans of time, was parallel to, but clearly distant from, the body that was painted, sculpted, and described. This insight and under-standing revealed to me the kind of critique which *Medical Nemesis* needed. At the core of my argument I had placed the art of living, the culturally shaped skill and will to live one's age, bearing or enduring and enjoying it. As a philosopher, I was interested in fostering and protecting this art and its traditions in a time of intensive medicalization of daily life. I tried to show that the art of living has both a sunny and a shadowy side; one can speak of an art of enjoyment and an art of suffering. On this point, I was criticized by some who questioned my motives in redefining 'culture' in a subjective way. My critics claimed that, by stressing the benefits of a culture that is the model for and the result of an 'art of suffering', I spoke as a romantic masochist, or as a preacher anxious to restrain any expectations of progress. Others applauded my attempt to root the concept of culture in the experienced meaning of personal suffering.

Body history, however, led me to see what was genuinely deficient in my analysis. Both enjoyment and suffering are abstract concepts. They name opposite forms in which sensations are culturally embodied. Enjoyment refers to the cultured incarnation of pleasure, and suffering to the topology of frustration, depression, anguish or pain. Each age has its style of experiencing the human condition that traditionally has been called 'the flesh.'

Until recently, I had looked at the body as a natural fact which stands outside the historian's domain. I had not understood the difference, which can be great, between the experienced body and other less ephemeral objects which the historian must examine for their use and meaning. My wonder at not finding a body like mine in the twelfth century led me to recognize the iatrogenic 'body' of the sixties as the result of a social construction which belonged to only one generation.

I realize that the medical system cannot engender a body, even if it cares for one from conception to brain death. In every epoch, bodies exist only in context. They form the felt equivalent of an age, in so far as that age can be experienced by a specific group. In most periods, women seem to have different kinds of bodies from men, serfs different from those of lords. It is the feel of the patient which tells the physician what to prescribe. The first to repair the new windmills which appeared in the thirteenth century, itinerant mechanics, were shunned by city and country folk alike because of their uncanny feel.

In the sociogenesis of our bodies, transportation plays as large a part as medicine does. Bodies which require daily shipment were unthinkable a few generations ago. We say that we 'go somewhere' when we drive or fly. Engineering manuals speak of 'self-transportation' when we use our feet rather than the elevator. And we feel entitled to high-tech crutches, deprived if we must fall back on our feet. I can understand the body of Americans during the period of the Vietnam war as belonging to *homo transportandus*, and carica-ture this body as the cancer-frightened consumer of valium. But after some study I see that the most apt terms must directly refer to a transition now taking place: the dissolution of the iatrogenic body into one fitted by and for high-tech. Choosing the adjective 'iatrogenic,' I call attention to the very special relationship between the medical establishment and body perception, a relationship which now dissolves before my eyes. I see something occurring.

Around the middle of this century, the medical establish-ment reached an unprecedented influence over the social construction of bodies. Designers deferred to medical norms in creating new furniture or automobiles; schools and the media inundated the imagination with medical and/or psy-chiatric fantasies; and the structures of welfare and insur-ance systems trained everyone for patienthood. We experienced a special moment of history when one agency, namely medicine, reached toward a monopoly over the social construction of bodily reality.

Usually the generation of the felt body cannot be assigned to just one agent. When the plague reached Florence in 1622–1623, no health care system was mobilized. In a remarkable study, Guilia Calvi describes how the entire city rose to the challenge of the scourge. Barbers and surgeons, together with candlemakers and smelling-salt vendors, mag-istrates and grave diggers, chaplains of special sanctuaries for desperate cases and incense merchants, each had their particular response to the epidemic. Each 'guild' was mobi-lized to become an 'antibody' of the plague. The flesh of each

Florentine, male or female, anguished or diseased, was caught, interpreted and reflected by different mirrors. No single professional body could by itself encompass the plagued flesh in a single mirror. No one agency was endorsed with the power to establish the felt body as such. The mid-twentieth century bid for such a monopoly on the part of medicine has been unprecedented and, as it turns out, shortlived.

I have come to believe that the medical establishment has lost this claim during the last ten years. Professional power over the definition of reality has reached its apogee and is now in decline. At this moment, a confusing mixture of high-tech and herbal wisdom, bio-engineering and autonomous exercise operate to create felt reality, including that of the body. Twenty years ago it was common to refer to 'the body I have' as 'my body.' We know that this reference to ownership in ordinary speech is post-Cartesian. It first appears in all European languages with the spread of possessive individualism, a phenomenon well described by C.B. McPherson. But now I frequently meet young people who smile when somebody does not 'identify' with his or her body. They speak of the body they 'are,' but then paradoxically, refer to it as 'my system.'

During the sixties the medical profession was prominent in determining what the body is and how it ought to feel. During the seventies it has begun to share with other agents the power to objectify people. From an enterprise that objectifies people as bodies or psyches, a new model has sprung up that engenders people who objectify themselves: those who conceive of themselves as 'producers' of their bodies. It is so far only a part of a new epistemological matrix which is in the process of formation. It may be one that brings forth people who experience themselves as contributors to a complex computer program, who see themselves as part of its text. Nothing seems to me more important now than the clear distinction between the current trend toward 'body building' and the traditional art of embodying culture.

The Institutional Construction of a New Fetish: Human Life

Presented as a 'Planning Event' of the
Evangelical Lutheran Church in America
Chicago, 29th March, 1989

Ladies and Gentlemen. On 1st January 1988, so you informed me, the Evangelical Lutheran Church of America came into existence. It is the result of a merger of three antecedent Churches. With 5.6 million members, it is the fourth largest Christian Church in the US. This Church and its Bishop have convoked a conference which you have labelled as a 'planning event.' I am one of half a dozen outsiders who have been invited to comment on the context in which the new Church's mission must respond.

I was asked to address something called 'resources and institutions.' I take up this challenge by making you reflect on a characteristic of twentieth-century institutions: their ability to generate entities that can be defined as basic needs and which, in turn, define resources that are perceived as being scarce. To illustrate my point I suggest that you look at the institutional relationship of the Church to a new kind of entity called 'life,' a notion variously referred to as '*a* life,' 'American lives,' 'human life on earth' and by some as 'gaya, the life of the biosphere.' These words are now frequently used in public discussion and refer to a new kind of social construct: an entity no one dares to think away. Analyzing this discourse I am led to the conclusion that entitative life, the subject of this new discourse, is spoken about as something precious, endangered, scarce. It is further spoken about as something amenable to institutional management, something which calls for the training of ever-new specialists from lab scientists to therapists and professional caretakers. Several Christian Churches claim an eminent responsibility as guardians of 'life,' or as specialists in its definition. On the other hand, 'life on Earth' plays the crucial role in the new mythology and philosophy of eco-sciences and is discussed as the ultimate resource to be protected. Life is an eminent example of an assumption that is convenient for the expansion of institutional control over resources which, by going unexamined, has taken on the features of a certainty.

I will present five historical observations to support my thesis. I will give to each of these the form of a mini-syllabus. This organization of my material in the form of conceptual units that could serve as outlines for a lecture or seminar makes it easier for you to conduct the discussion for which you have invited me. It also suggests the lines for a historical and theological research project. The Lutheran Church to which we owe the leadership in the field of Biblical studies might take the lead in exploring the relationship between life in the Bible and what the term is used to mean now.

Philip Hefner asked me for a forceful presentation to generate theological response and issue-oriented discussion of concrete subjects. So I begin by stating a thesis:

> 'Human life' is a recent social construct, something which we now take so much for granted that we dare not seriously question it. I propose that the Church exorcize references to the new substantive life from its own discourse.

Life constitutes an essential referent in current ecological, medical, legal, political and ethical discourse. Consistently those who use it forget that the notion has a history; it is a Western notion, ultimately the result of a perversion of the Christian message. And it is also a highly contemporary notion, with confusing connotations that obliterate the power of the word to denote anything precise. Thinking in terms of 'a life' and 'human life' vaguely connotes something of extreme importance and tends to abolish all limits that decency and common sense have so far imposed on the exercise of professional tutelage.

As currently used, the English words 'life' and '*a* life' feed the most powerful idol which the Church has had to face in the course of her history. More than the ideology of empire or feudal order, more than nationalism or progress, more than gnosticism or enlightenment, the acceptance of substantive life as a God-given reality lends itself to a new corruption of the Christian faith. What I fear is this: that the Churches, due to a lack of firm rooting in Biblical language, engage the myth-making power which they possess as late twentieth century institutions to foster, consecrate and sanctify the abstract secular notion of 'life.' Carrying out this profoundly 'religious' and equally non-Christian enterprise, they thereby make it possible that this spectral entity progressively replace the notion of 'person' in which the humanism of Western individualism is anchored. '*A* Life' is amenable to management, to improvement and to evaluation in terms of available resources in a way which is unthinkable when we speak of '*a* person.'

Paralysis of language in a managed world

I am turning the idea of management into a key problem of the encounter between Church and World. I do so because it is through management that those certainties are shaped and confirmed for the sake of which our late twentieth century society is organized. I want to call your attention to the dangers rather than to the opportunities of the Church co-sponsoring these realities in collaboration with other institutions.

The difficulty of addressing you on this particular subject appears in every sentence of the mail about this conference which I have been sent during the last seven months. Let me illustrate by caricature. In the first paragraph of the first letter you speak about a Church which 'came into existence' not on Pentecost, but on January 1st. You inform us that this Church resulted not from the will of God but from a merger of three antecedent institutions. This Church has a bishop, but one surrounded by an executive staff, a team which organizes itself for planning. With touching innocence the Vatican-like agencies of the eighties present themselves in managerial terms. Now, I am not challenging the necessity of competent accounting, banking, window cleaning and fund raising. I am not even questioning public relations, statistics and lobbying. And I welcome calling a spade what it is. But the *innocence* with which Church people apply to their community metaphors taken from corporations deserves some attention. Let me tell you a story.

One of my great teachers was Jacques Maritain, philosopher, neo-thomist, mystical poet and, at the time of the story, a colleague of Einstein at the Institute of Advanced Studies in Princeton. It was 1957, the second year after my transfer from a slum parish in New York to educational administration in Puerto Rico. I had become deeply involved in the newly established manpower qualification planning board of the island's Government. I was deeply upset by the philosophical ambiguities into which planning, *not* of the Church, but of something called *qualified manpower* was leading me. Dictionaries did not help me: 'planning' does not appear in the pre-war supplement to the Oxford English Dictionary though it was launched within the same couple of years by Hitler, Stalin and Roosevelt. So on my next visit to the mainland I went to see Professor Maritain, who had earlier guided my studies on the history of the practice and theory of virtue in the Christian West. How could I fit 'planning' into the traditional system of responsible habits within which I had learned to think? I had great difficulty in explaining to the old man the meaning of the term that I was using: planning was not accounting, nor was it legislation, nor a kind of scheduling of trains. We took tea on his veranda. It was to be my last visit with him. I was delighted to look at his beautiful face, close to death, transparent, like one of the patriarchs in a Gothic stained glass window. The cup in his hand was shaking. Then, finally, he put it down, looking disturbed, and said: 'Is not planning, which you talk about, a sin, a new species within the vices which grow out of presumption?' He made me understand that in thinking about humans as resources that can be managed, a new certitude about human nature would be brought into existence surreptitiously.

Today it would seem silly to examine the notion of planning within the context of Christian virtues. Planning long ago acquired the public status of an accepted and well-tested technique. Today, it has become quite unthinkable to question the epistemic status of notions like 'management,' 'control,' 'communication,' 'professionalism' and other related ideas. With the semblance of understanding, speakers recklessly apply these concepts to almost anything in any way the speaker chooses. For instance, once 'manpower' has become the object of research, planning, development, investment and improvement, the ghost of manpower takes on the features of a compact reality. Even children learn to think in terms of *human resources*. Their popular games inculcate policies, programs, decision-making. Throughout life the concept of scarce resources in need of management acquires the guise of a-historical certainty. The ominous power of modern institutions consists in their ability to create and to name the social reality which the institutions' experts need as the substance they manage.

The power of management to *name* norms of health, education, psychic balance, development and other modern idols is no less important than its power to actually create the social context within which a default in regard to these 'values' is experienced as a *need* which in turn translates into an entitlement. This point is of particular importance within the tradition of the Lutheran Church, with its intense awareness of the Church's duty to announce the Word of God. The evangelical critique of the universe of bureaucratic terminology which penetrates and colors everyday conversation and consciousness seems to me a God-given task implied in one's witness to the Word of God.

Epistemic sentimentality

The day-by-day experience of a managed existence leads us

all to take a world of fictitious substances for granted. It leads us to speak about these managed phantoms with new words like 'progress' in health care, universal education, global consciousness, social development; with words that suggest something 'better,' 'scientific,' 'modern,' 'advanced,' 'beneficial to the poor.' The verbal amoebas by which we designate the management-bred phantoms thus connote self-important enlightenment, social concern and rationality without however denoting anything which we could ourselves taste, smell or experience. In this semantic desert full of muddled echoes we need a Linus blanket, some prestigious fetish that we can drag around to feel like decent defenders of sacred values. Social justice at home, development overseas and world peace appear in retrospect as such fetishes; the new fetish is Life. There is something apocalyptic to search for life under a microscope (Mt.24,26).

There are people who are pro-life: some oppose abortion, others vivisection, capital punishment or war. Their opponents want the choice to interrupt pregnancy or life-saving treatment. As Will Campbell said to me three years ago: 'life is tearing the Church apart.' And yet, no one dares to oppose the use of this verbal amoeba in public controversy. Least of all churchmen. Some burn incense to life. Others have become specialists in peddling pseudo-biblical pieties about the 'value' of life. While Medicine manages life from sperm to worm, Churches have acquired a new social standing by framing these medical activities within the semblance of an ethical discourse. Bio-ethics provides a new and prestigious job market which gives preference to unemployed clerics with university degrees. I am therefore fully aware of the difficulty I face when I choose life as my exemplary instance of a notion which takes on spectral but unquestioned existence through an institutional commitment to new domains of management. And I am also aware of an added hazard: I present this example to a Church which resulted from a merger last January 1st, and whose executives are anxious to know what the world expects from their institution.

I can tell you: the Christian West has given birth to a radically different kind of human condition, unlike anything that has ever existed or that could have come into existence without the Church's millennial midwifery. Only within the matrix which Jacques Ellul calls the 'technological system' has this new type of human condition come to full fruition. A new role opens for mythmaking, moralizing, legitimizing institutions, a role which cannot quite be understood in terms of old religions, but which some churches rush in to fill.

The new technological society is singularly incapable of generating myths to which people can form deep and rich attachments. Yet, for its rudimentary maintenance it needs agencies which create legitimate fetishes to which epistemic sentimentality can attach itself. At no previous time was there a similar demand for agencies capable of rendering such a service. And the major Christian Churches — traditionally legitimate, intellectually prestigious, well managed, independently financed — appear as apt centers to be entrusted with this task. The Gorbachev epoch is not one in which the Church faces Jacobins. Rather, a new kind of conspiracy threatens: not with the triumphalism of a Constantinian empire, but with powers that promote welfare, development and justice as the means of maintaining order and peace.

The Gospel of Life

I was not taught to believe that the Church finds its vocation by listening to the world. The Lutheran Church is not only populous and rich; not only one of the important agencies defining moral issues in public life and speaking out for ethical responsibility in American politics; not only one of the key institutions providing social coherence, along with orchestras, democratic clubs, alumni associations and the Daughters of the American Revolution. I cannot but believe that it is also and, above all, one of the major vessels to which a distinctive theological tradition has been entrusted. All American Christians are in some way dependent on the Lutheran Church safeguarding Gospel words in a world full of pop-science junk terms. The clear discrimination between *the* Life and *a* life is today an essential and paradigmatic part of this task. But, how can we demand that the Church anathematize an idol at the very moment when she has lost her ability to define the terms she uses to announce her own message? How to demand that the Church sail against the very current into which she steered the West?

The comparison between the Church and an ocean-going sailing vessel goes back to patristic times. It antedates the invention of the central rudder and the ominous connotations of control which this image suggests. The unwieldy vessel now sails through utterly strange waters, those which medieval maps show at the edge of the world, where the oceans burn, and heavens rain sulphur. I can think of no better picture to evoke for you what it means to be the crew of a Church in the 1990s, when the elements through which generations have sailed have almost disappeared: ozone and climate, genetic variety and hereditary immunities, forests and whales — that is, more importantly, the cedars that give the Salomonic Temple its sensual quality, the monster in whose belly Jonas, like Christ, spent three days.

It is in these regions of dissimilitude that you find yourselves huddled together for a week of prayerful reflection, carrying on board the Good News which the Lord announces to Martha when he says to her 'I am Life.' He does not say, 'I am a life.' He says, 'I am Life,' *tout court*. Hypostatic life has its historical roots in the revelation that one human person, Jesus, is also God. This one Life is the substance of Martha's faith, and of ours. We hope to receive this Life as a gift, and we hope to share it. We know that this Life was given to us on the Cross, and that we cannot seek it except on the *via crucis*. To be merely alive does not yet mean having this Life. This Life is gratuitous, beyond and above having been born and living. But, as Augustine and Luther constantly stress, it is a gift without which being alive would be as dust.

This Life is personal to the point of *being* one person, both revealed and promised in John 19. This life is something profoundly other than the life which appears as a substantive in the headlines of US newspapers. And at first sight, the two have nothing in common. On one side, the word says: Emmanuel, God-man, Incarnation. On the other, the term is used to impute substance to a process for which the physician assumes responsibility, which technologies prolong and atomic armaments protect; which has standing in court, can be wrongfully given; a process about whose destruction, without due procedure or beyond the needs of national defense or industrial growth, so-called pro-life organizations are incensed.

However, on closer inspection, life as a property, as a value, a national resource, a right, is a Western notion which shares its Christian ancestry with other key verities defining secular society. The notion of an entitative human life which can be professionally and legally protected has been tortuously construed through a legal-medical-religious-scientific discourse whose roots go far back into theology. The emotional and conceptual connotations of life in the Hindu, Buddhist or Islamic traditions are utterly distinct from those evident in the current discourse on this subject in Western democracies. This is a primary reason why the demystification of life is a service in which theologically-trained historians ought to engage.

Politically, pro-life movements are sponsored mainly by Christian denominations. And these organizations have played a major role in the social construction of the idol of which I speak. This is a second reason why I look to the Church to clarify the notion. The Christian Churches now face an ugly temptation: to cooperate in the social creation of a fetish which, in a theological perspective, is the perversion of revealed Life into an idol.

Five observations on the history of life

Christian theology starts where iconoclasm has done its job. If as an *institution* you put your *resources* into an interpretation of the Gospel that tries to shun epistemic sentimentality, the 'history of life' belongs on your agenda. And those who engage in this history might well keep five points in mind.

First, life, as a substantive notion, makes its appearance around 1801.

Biblical scholars are well aware of the limited correspondence between the Hebrew word for blood, *dam*, and the Greek term we would render as soul, namely, *psyché*. Neither comes anywhere near the meaning of the substantive, *life*. The concept of life does not exist in Greco-Roman antiquity: *bios* means the course of a destiny and *zoe* something close to the brilliance of aliveness. In Hebrew, the concept is utterly theo-centric, an implication of God's breath.

Life as a substantive notion appears 2000 years later, along with the science that purports to study it. The term 'biology' was coined early in the nineteenth century by Jean-Baptiste Lamarck. He was reacting to the Baroque progress in botany and zoology which tended to reduce these two disciplines to the status of mere classification. By inventing a new term, he also named a new field of study, 'the science of life.'

Lamarck's genius confronted the tradition of distinct vegetable and animal ensoulment, along with the consequent division of nature into three kingdoms: mineral, vegetable and animal. He postulated the existence of life that distinguishes living beings from inorganic matter, not by visible structure but by organization. Since Lamarck, biology searches for the 'stimulating cause of organization' and its localization in tissues, cells, protoplasm, the genetic code or morphogenetic fields. 'What is life?' is, therefore, not a perennial question but the pop-science counterfoil to scientific research reports on a mixed bag of phenomena such as reproduction, physiology, heredity, organization, evolution and, more recently, feedback and morphogenesis. Life appears during the Napoleonic wars as a postulate which is meant to lead the new biologists beyond the competing descriptive studies of mechanists, vitalists and materialists. Then, as morphological, physiological and genetic studies became more precise towards the middle of the nineteenth century, life and its evolution become the hazy and unintended by-products reflecting in ordinary discourse an increasingly abstract and formal kind of scientific terminology. With the possible exception of the earliest two generations of nineteenth century biologists, *obiter dicta* based upon the substantive notion of life are not, and never have been, part of the argument of biology as a science. It is therefore surprising to observe with what solemnity biologists have recently been asked by church executives to pool their competence with that of theologians in the study of issues related to post-Lamarckian life.

Second, the loss of contingency, the death of nature and the appearance of life are but distinct aspects of the same new consciousness.

A thread which runs back to Anaxagoras (500–428 B.C.) links a number of otherwise profoundly distinct philosophical systems: the theme of nature's aliveness. This idea of nature's sensitive responsiveness found its constant expression well into the sixteenth century in animistic and idealistic, gnostic and hylomorphic versions. In these variations, nature is experienced as the matrix from which all things are born. In the long period between Augustine and Scotus this birthing power of nature was rooted in the world's being *contingent* on the incessant creative will of God. By the thirteenth century, and especially in the Franciscan school of theology, the world's being is seen as contingent not merely on God's creation, but also on the graceful sharing of His own being, His life. Whatever is brought from possibility, *de potentia*, into the necessity of its own existence thrives by its miraculous sharing in God's own intimacy, for which there is no better word than — His Life.

With the scientific revolution, contingency-rooted thought fades, and a mechanistic model comes to dominate perception. Caroline Merchant argues that the resulting 'death of nature' has been *the* most far-reaching event in changing men's vision and perception of the universe. But it also raised the nagging question: how to explain the existence of living forms in a dead cosmos? The notion of substantive life thus appears not as a direct answer to this question, but as a kind of mindless shibboleth to fill a void.

Third, the ideology of possessive individualism has shaped the way life could be talked about as a property.

Since the nineteenth century, the legal construction of society increasingly reflects a new philosophical radicalism in the perception of the self. The result is a break with the ethics which had informed Western history since Greek antiquity, clearly expressed by the shift of concern from *the good* to *values*. Society is now organized on the utilitarian assumption that man is born needy, and needed values are by definition scarce. The possession of life in axiology is then interpreted as the supreme value. *Homo œconomicus* becomes the referent for ethical reflection. Living is equated with a struggle for survival or, more radically, with a competition for life. For over a century now it has become customary to speak about the 'conservation of life' as the ultimate motive of human action and social organization. Today, some bio-ethicists go even further. While up to now the law implied that a person was alive, *they* demand that we recognize that there is a deep difference between having a life and merely being alive. The proven ability to exercise this act of possession or appropriation is turned into the criterion for 'personhood' and for the existence of a legal subject.

During this same period, *homo œconomicus* was surreptitiously taken as the emblem and analog for all living beings. A mechanistic anthropomorphism has gained currency. Bacteria are imagined to mimic 'economic' behavior and to engage in internecine competition for the scarce oxygen available in their environment. A cosmic struggle among ever more complex forms of life has become the anthropic foundational myth of the scientific age.

Fourth, the factitious nature of life appears with special poignancy in ecological discussion.

Ecology can mean the study of correlations between living forms and their habitat. The term is also and increasingly used for a philosophical way of correlating all knowable phenomena. It then signifies thinking in terms of a cybernetic system which, in real time, is both model and reality: a process which observes and defines, regulates and sustains itself. Within this style of thinking, life comes to be equated with *the* system: it is the abstract fetish that both overshadows and simultaneously constitutes it.

Epistemic sentimentality has its roots in this conceptual collapse of the borderline between cosmic process and substance, and the mythical embodiment of both in the fetish of life. Being conceived as a sytem, the cosmos is imagined in analogy to an entity which can be rationally analyzed and managed. Simultaneously, this very same abstract mechanism is romantically identified with life and spoken about in hushed tones as something mysterious, polymorphic, weak, demanding tender protection. In a new kind of reading, Genesis now tells how Adam and Eve were entrusted with life and the further improvement of its quality. This new Adam is potter and nurse of the Golem.

Fifth, the pop-science fetish 'a' life tends to void the legal notion of person.

This process is well illustrated in the relationship between medical practice, juridical proceedings and bio-ethical discourse. Physicians in the Hippocratic tradition were bound to restore the balance (health) of their patient's constitution, and forbidden to use their skills to deal with death. They had to accept nature's power to dissolve the healing contract between the patient and his physician. When the Hippocratic signs indicated to the physician that the patient had entered into agony, the 'atrium between life and death,' he had to withdraw from what was now a deathbed. Quickening — which means coming alive — in the womb and the onset of agony — a personal struggle to die — defined the extreme boundaries between which a subject of medical care could be conceived. This now rapidly changes. Physicians are taught to consider themselves responsible for lives from the moment the egg is fertilized through the time of organ harvest. In the early twentieth century, the physician came to be perceived as society's appointed tutor of any person who, having been placed in the patient role, lost some of his own competence. Now he becomes the socially responsible manager not of a patient, but of a life. According to one of the most reputable bio-ethicists, science has endowed society with the ability to distinguish between a life which is that of a human person and that which corresponds to 'a human non-person.' The latter creature lacks the quality or 'capacity required to play a role in the moral community.' The new discipline of bio-ethics mediates between pop science and law by creating the semblance of a moral discourse that roots 'personhood' in the qualitative evaluation of the fetish, life.

Medical Ethics: A Call to De-bunk Bio-ethics

Drafted with Dr Robert Mendelsohn
for discussion at the School of Medicine,
University of Illinois
Chicago, 20th November 1987

Medical ethics is an oxymoron, bringing to mind safe sex, nuclear protection and military intelligence.

Since 1970, bio-ethics has spread like an epidemic, creating the semblance of ethical choice in an intrinsically unethical context. This context has taken its shape from the extension of medicine from conception to organ harvest. Given this new domain of operation, medicine has ceased to look at the sufferings of a sick person: the object of care has become something called a human life.

The transmogrification of a person into 'a life' is a lethal operation, as dangerous as reaching out for the tree of life in the time of Adam and Eve.

Ethics, institutes, programs and courses have created a discourse within which 'life' appears as the object of medical, professional and administrative management. Thus, the umbrella of academic rationalization is now lending legitimacy to an essentially flawed enterprise. Medical ethics now obscures the practice of virtue in suffering and dying.

We consider bio-ethics irrelevant to the aliveness with which we intend to face pain and anguish, renunciation and death.

Other works by Ivan Illich available from Marion Boyars Publishers

---

CELEBRATION OF AWARENESS

This, his first book, established Ivan Illich as a formidable and passionate critic of the social myths and cherished institutions of modern industrial society. Committed to a radical humanism he set himself the target of breaking down the ideologies which alienate men from men as well as from their traditional sources of human dignity and joy. The author challenges newer orthodoxies and current ideas of social virtue by his profound questioning of bourgeois and liberal assumptions. He urges us to a new celebration of awareness so that we can escape the existing dehumanizing systems by our unwillingness to be constrained and our willingness to accept responsibility for the future.

DESCHOOLING SOCIETY

Ivan Illich presents a startling view of schooling: schooling (as opposed to education) has become our modern dogma, a sacred cow which all must worship, serve, and submit to, yet from which little true nourishment is derived. Schools have failed our individual needs, supporting fallacious notions of 'progress' and development that follow from the belief that ever-increasing production, consumption and profit are proper yardsticks for measuring the quality of human life. Our schools have become recruiters of personnel for the consumer society, certifying citizens for service, while at the same time disposing of those adjudged unfit for the competitive race. The author offers radical suggestions for reform.

TOOLS FOR CONVIVIALITY

A work of seminal importance, this book presents the author's penetrating analysis of the industrial mode of production where enterprises, ranging from health services to national defense, are 'each producing a service commodity, each organized as a public utility and each defining its output as a basic necessity', and eventually imposing their uses on the consumer. Illich chooses 'conviviality' to mean the opposite: 'individual freedom realized in personal interdependence and, as such, an intrinsic ethical value'. The overall objective is to survive with justice, avoiding the bleak prospects of totally planned goals and desires and total loss of individual privacy.

ENERGY AND EQUITY

In this essay, by means of a detailed survey of the way people travel, Ivan Illich develops his arguments against industrial society. He argues that speed is a source and tool of political manipulative power in rich as well as poor countries. The ideology of continual growth of both socialist and capitalist systems imposes intolerable social inequalities. The overconsumption of energy not only destroys the physical environment through pollution but causes the disintegration of society itself. Illich advocates a radical political decision to neutralize the energy crisis by the limiting of traffic, which he argues corrupts and enslaves, and results in a further decline of equity, leisure and autonomy for all.

LIMITS TO MEDICINE
Medical Nemesis – The Expropriation of Health.

'The medical establishment has become a major threat to health'. This is the opening statement and basic contention of Ivan Illich's searing social critique. Decimating the myth of the magic of contemporary medicine and ruthlessly examining the rituals conducted by the medical profession and its adjuncts, he demonstrates how the fulfilment of genuine human needs, such as the maintenance of good health, has been turned by over-professionalization into a nightmarish spiritual and physical agent of destruction: treatment creates illness. In response Illich calls for a halt to the expropriation of man's coping ability and presents an alternative to the inevitable Medical Nemesis that will set in unless the autonomy of the individual is re-established.

DISABLING PROFESSIONS

Ivan Illich, Irving Kenneth Zola, John McKnight,
Jonathan Caplan, Harley Shaiken
Why do we spend so much on health services, and levels of treatment do not improve? Why do we spend so much on education and our children seem to learn less? Why is so much spent on law enforcement and criminal justice systems and our society seems less secure and less just? This fascinating and controversial collection of essays questions the power of the professional over an apathetic citizenry.

THE RIGHT TO USEFUL UNEMPLOYMENT
AND ITS PROFESSIONAL ENEMIES

Here Ivan Illich, possibly at his most controversial, calls for the right to *useful* unemployment: a positive, constructive, and even optimistic concept dealing with that activity by which people are useful to themselves and others *outside* the production of commodities for the market. Unfettered by managing professionals, unmeasured and unmeasurable by economists, these activities truly generate satisfaction, creativity and freedom.

SHADOW WORK

This major historical and sociological analysis of modern man's economic existence traces and analyzes options which surpass the conventional political 'right-left' and the technological 'soft-hard' alternatives and presents the concept of the 'vernacular' domain: 'the preparation of food and the shaping of language, childbirth and recreation.' Illich deals provocatively with the controlling uses of language and science and the valuation of women and work.

GENDER

Ivan Illich insists that we survey attitudes to male and female in both industrial society and its antecedents in order to recover a lost 'art of living'. In pre-industrial communities there was 'vernacular gender': the sexes accepted their differences which were expressed in speech-idioms and apportioned tasks. The increasingly powerful forces of organized religion, and the rise of a commercial culture, created images of the sexes which acquired self-perpetuating power. Our present industrial society has debased 'vernacular gender' into 'economic sex' — less secure and more savagely crippling. Illich argues that only a radical scrutiny of scarcity can prevent an intensification of this grim predicament.

H_2O AND THE WATERS OF FORGETFULNESS

'Water throughout history has been perceived as the stuff which radiates purity: H_2O is the new stuff, on whose purification human survival now depends. H_2O and water have become opposites: H_2O is a social creation of modern times, a resource that is scarce and that calls for technical management. It is an observed fluid that has lost the ability to mirror the water of dreams'. Tracing the history of the use and abuse of H_2O as a source of commodity in twentieth century life with its quest for odorless hygiene, Ivan Illich contrasts these matters with an examination of the history of ideas, mythologies and visions associated with water.

ABC: THE ALPHABETIZATION OF THE POPULAR MIND
(with Barry Sanders)

Ivan Illich and Barry Sanders (medieval scholar and literary critic) have produced an original and provocative study of the advent, spread and present decline of literacy. They explore the impact of the alphabet on fundamental thought processes and attitudes and culminate their research in an examination of the present erosion of literacy in the new technological languages of 'newspeak' and 'uniquack'; and they point out how new attitudes to language are altering our worldview, our sense of self and of community.